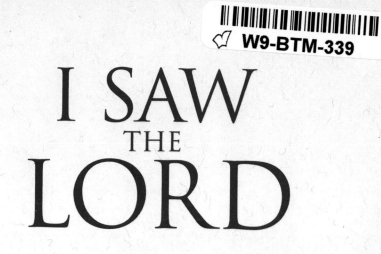

I SAW
THE
LORD

I SAW
THE
LORD

A WAKE-UP CALL FOR YOUR HEART

ANNE
GRAHAM
LOTZ

ZONDERVAN.com/
AUTHORTRACKER
follow your favorite authors

◼ ZONDERVAN®

I Saw the Lord
Copyright © 2006 by Anne Graham Lotz

This title is also available as a Zondervan audio product.
Visit www.zondervan.com/audiopages for more information.

Requests for information should be addressed to:

Zondervan, *Grand Rapids, Michigan 49530*

Library of Congress Cataloging-in-Publication Data

Lotz, Anne Graham, 1948–
    I saw the Lord : a wake-up call for your heart / Anne Graham Lotz.
       p. cm.
    Includes bibliographical references.
    ISBN-13: 978-0-310-28470-3 (softcover)
    ISBN-10: 0-310-28470-8 (softcover)
    1. Bible. O.T. Isaiah VI—Criticism, interpretation, etc. I. Title.
BS1515.52.L68 2005
242'.5—dc22
                                       2005030104

Published in association with the literary agency of Alive Communications, Inc., 7680 Goddard St., Suite 200, Colorado Springs, CO 80920.

Interior design by Beth Shagene

Printed in the United States of America

---

07 08 09 10 11 12 • 22 21 20 19 18 17 16 15 14 13 12 11 10 9 8 7 6 5 4 3 2 1

*Dedicated
to
the church.*

My eyes have seen the King, the Lord Almighty.

ISAIAH 6:5

Contents

With My Gratitude Forever
to the
Wake-up Callers,
the *Just Give Me Jesus*
2000 – 2005
Revival Team Chairs,
women who have answered the call to personal revival
and poured their lives into issuing that call to others:

Ann Furrow, Dee Haslam, Donna Cobble
Knoxville, Tennessee

Janet Denison
Dallas – Fort Worth, Texas

Mary Frances Bowley, Karen Loritts
Atlanta, Georgia

Marilyn Thomas
Kansas City, Missouri

Darlene Barber
San Diego, California

Dana Iverson, Sue Asp, Nancy Perkins
Fargo, North Dakota

Myrl Glockner
Minneapolis – St. Paul, Minnesota

Michelle Yount
Phoenix, Arizona

Laura Caison, Mary Marchman
Raleigh, North Carolina

Barbara Widdoes, Katie Williams
Cleveland, Ohio

Deborah Harris, Marilyn Chambers
Charlotte, North Carolina

Verna Pauls
Denver, Colorado

Heather Gills, Trisha Emerson, Cheryl Anderson, Debbie Christensen
Tampa, Florida

Sue McGee, Rosz Akins
Lexington, Kentucky

Dr. Rhee Kwangja, Dr. Chung Hwak Sil
Seoul, South Korea

Sheena Gillies, Margaret McVeigh, Jean Wilson
London, England

Elizabeth McQuoid, Juliet Lloyd
Cardiff, Wales

Bethsaida Lamar
San Juan, Puerto Rico

Pam MacRae
Chicago, Illinois

Doris Gillett, Valerie Vicknair, Colleen Nordlund
Seattle, Washington

Lucia Bergen, Anita Neufeld, Maria Gloria Duarte
Asunción, Paraguay

Shirley Barber, Naomi Cox, Marge Ainley
Fresno, California

Kitty Proctor, Mary Selzer
Detroit, Michigan

Nadezhda Komendant
Kiev, Ukraine

A Wake-up Call

I had been speaking in back-to-back sessions for three days, and that
night I collapsed into bed, dead to the world before my head even hit
the pillow ...

Eventually the brilliant rays of the not-so-early morning sunlight
coming through the blinds pried my sleeping eyes open. As I lay in
bed, enjoying the warmth under the down comforter, my mind began
to stir before my body did. My first thought was, *Why is the sun up so
early?* Then my body stirred, and I rolled over to look at the clock. It
said 7:30! For a moment I lay in a stunned stupor — then I hit the floor
with a muffled, "Oh no!"

I was scheduled to lead the final morning sessions of my intensive
seminar at The Billy Graham Training Center at The Cove at 8:00! And
the final sessions involved not only my giving a sixty-minute message
followed by a commitment service, but it also involved my leading
communion for the first time!

Grabbing the clock, I violently shook it and silently demanded, *Why
didn't you go off? Now there's no time to prepare for all I have to do this
morning! There's not even time to get dressed! I shouldn't have relied on
you, you stupid clock! I should have asked for a wake-up call instead!*

Have you ever slept through your alarm? Or found out too late that it
didn't go off because you had mistakenly set it for p.m. instead of a.m.?
I will never forget the sick feeling I had that morning at The Cove when

my alarm, for whatever reason, did not function. I had peacefully slept on and on and on, oblivious to what time it was.

I have learned the hard way that I need wake-up calls when I'm on the road in ministry so I don't miss something important. But from time to time, I also need them in my own life. The daily routine of responsibilities, the never-ending challenge of deadlines, the persistent pressure of problems, and the hectic pace of everyday life tend to preoccupy my thoughts and time with the urgency of the moment. If I'm not careful, I may miss something vital that God has for me — something He may want me to see or do, some blessing He wants to give me or someone else.

I believe this kind of vital message was delivered during the week of August 29, 2005. Two days before it made landfall, a category 1 hurricane suddenly exploded into a category 5 over the exceptionally warm waters of the Gulf of Mexico. Her name was Katrina, and she came ashore that Monday morning just east of New Orleans, effectively eradicating anything and everything for hundreds of miles. The human misery she left in her wake was described as a disaster of biblical proportions. Entire towns were turned into heaps of rubble. Oil rigs broke off their moorings and crashed inland, looking like displaced Eiffel Towers rising up out of garbage dumps. Boats were in the tops of trees, houses were swept into the sea, cars were submerged in swimming pools, dead bodies floated down city streets, and everywhere … *everywhere!* … there was not only the overwhelming stench of death but also the stench of fear and grief, helplessness and hopelessness, desperation and despair.

Hurricane Katrina was a resounding wake-up call, not just to New Orleans and the Gulf Coast, but to this entire nation. *Wake up, America! Disaster can strike at any moment! Your unprecedented prosperity, your advanced technology, your shock-and-awe military do not guarantee you immunity from death, disease, despair, and sudden devastation. God's past blessings do not mean that He will keep you safe at present or in the future. Your hope is not in the local or state or federal government. Your hope is in the Lord alone. With all your know-how and your go-to-it innovative, creative ideas, you cannot predict your future or secure your future. God holds your future, and you need to get right with Him.*

Do you think America heard the wake-up call?

Jesus told a parable that came to my mind as I watched news reports of hurricane parties on Bourbon Street in the French Quarter of New Orleans that were held the night before Katrina made landfall. Jesus described a rich man who produced a good crop and then said to himself, "'You have plenty of good things laid up for many years. Take life easy; eat, drink and be merry.' But God said to him, 'You fool! This very night your life will be demanded from you.'"[1]

Several days after the storm and the flood that occurred when the levees that protected New Orleans broke, news sources reported that some bars still remained opened on Bourbon Street. And a previously scheduled gay pride parade was held as planned. Added to the organized parade and businesses, there were hundreds of individuals who looted and even shot at rescuers as anarchy reigned within the city. The atmosphere was one of defiance of any accountability or moral code as little dust people shook their little dust fists in God's face, turning deaf ears to what surely was a wake-up call.

As I write this, Hurricane Rita, another devastating storm, has hurled massive destruction upon an even wider area of the Gulf Coast. Yet as millions fled in front of Rita's powerful threat, the first business that is reported to have officially reopened in the French Quarter of New Orleans is a strip club that has expressed the desire to do its part by "entertaining" the weary firefighters and police officers of the city.

While tears flooded my eyes and my heart ached for the helpless, homeless, hopeless people whose entire lives were devastated along the Gulf Coast, I wondered how it could be that so many people apparently slept — and are still sleeping — through such a loud wake-up call!

What about you? Did you hear the wake-up call in the reverberating thunder of bomb blasts echoing throughout London streets? Or in the sharp explosion followed that left tangled cars and human carnage in Madrid train stations? Or in the roar of thirty-foot waves that brought sudden death and sweeping destruction to South Asia?

Maybe the wake-up call in some way needs to be directly personal before we can hear it ...

For me, God's wake-up call came in the attack on America on September 11, 2001. I had been peacefully "sleeping" through my routine of family and ministry, faithfully fulfilling my obligations and responsibilities. Without realizing it, I had been lulled into something of a complacent, passive attitude toward things that may not have been pressing issues at the moment but were of preeminent importance in the big scheme of things.

When the telephone rang that Tuesday morning, I heard my youngest daughter's anxious voice urging me to turn on the television because a plane had flown into one of the World Trade Center towers in New York City. Thinking some small, single-engine plane had somehow lost its way, I was unprepared for what appeared on the screen. Sitting in the quiet, serene beauty of my comfortable sunroom, I watched in stunned horror as the first tower erupted in flames like a gigantic butane torch. Then, unbelievably, a second plane hit the second tower! As the television cameras panned over the chaotic scene and followed the rush of emergency personnel to the stricken area, the reporter's voice lost its professional tone, and he yelled, "The tower is coming down!"

Within what seemed like moments frozen in time, in a scene straight out of hell, the first tower imploded, followed by the second tower. Suddenly the television screen was split. On one side I could see the mushroom cloud of smoke and dust and debris rising ominously from Lower Manhattan; on the other side I could see a section of the Pentagon in flames. And then, as the announcer was reporting that a plane had flown at jet speed into the Pentagon, a third picture revealed a smoldering crater in a Pennsylvania field where yet a fourth plane had nose-dived into the earth, disintegrating on impact and killing everyone on board.

Tears streamed down my cheeks, my heart broke, and I heard my own voice crying out, "Oh, God, no! No! So many people dying! Right now! God, help them!" As I sat transfixed with my eyes glued to the television screen, I knew people at that moment were stepping into eternity, and I wondered, *How many people went to work this morning, parked their cars, rode up the elevators, unlocked their office doors, booted up their computers, poured a cup of coffee, and reached for the telephone ... then in the blink of an eye, found themselves in eternity, standing before God?!*

My next thought was, *How many of those people stepping into eternity right now are not ready to meet God?*

Then the wake-up call came: *Anne, how many of those people are stepping into eternity, unprepared to meet God, because people like you have been so politically correct that no one has ever told them ...*

that God loves them,

that He wants them to live with Him forever in His heavenly home,

that He has given His own Son, Jesus, to be their Savior,

that through faith in Him they could have ...

forgiveness of sin,

a right relationship with God,

peace in their hearts,

and the confident hope of eternal life?

On that day, God woke me up and set my heart on fire to tell other people the glorious good news of the gospel of Jesus Christ: that through faith in Jesus, regardless of what happens in this life, we can be safe forever. Soon after 9/11, He used this personal wake-up call to open my eyes to the desperate need for a larger, broader, more far-reaching wake-up call ... within the church.

The need for the wake-up call to the church came sharply into focus several days after 9/11 when I was invited to participate in a national television news program. *The Early Show* on CBS originated in New York City, but I was able to interact with co-host Jane Clayson by a remote connection to a site in the city where I live.

The morning of the interview, I found myself seated alone in a small broadcast studio facing the cold, impersonal stare of a camera lens. Brilliant lights that were pointed in my direction revealed every stray hair on my head, every blemish on my face, and every wrinkle on my skin. The earpiece in my left ear crackled with static as a voice asked me to count to five for a sound check of the microphone that was clipped discreetly to my lapel. As I complied, I was struck with how small my voice sounded in the dead air of what felt like a concrete cell crisscrossed with cables, flooded with high-intensity lighting, and now tense with anticipation of going on the air live before millions of people that made up the show's national television audience.

The dramatic sounds of the production crew's urgent communication coming through my earpiece alerted me that the program I was to participate in was coming out of a commercial break. With no monitor to distract my focus from the camera lens and therefore no visual image of the person to whom I would be speaking, I heard Jane Clayson introduce me briefly, then the interview began:

CLAYSON: Mrs. Lotz, we've turned to your father, the Reverend Billy Graham, so often in times of national crisis. What are his thoughts about what happened on Tuesday?

LOTZ: I called him last night after you all had called to arrange for this. And he's reacting like a lot of Christians around the country. We're all praying. I know the families and friends of the victims can hardly even pray for themselves. They don't know what to say or how to pray. And I want to say to them, that there are thousands of people in this country who are carrying you in prayer right now. And we're praying for you with hearts filled with compassion and grief, asking the God of all peace and the God of all comfort to come down in a special way into your life and meet your needs at this time. My father and my mother are also praying like that.

CLAYSON: The pain is incomprehensible for so many of these people, and at a time like this, it's so easy to lose faith. How do you keep faith, Mrs. Lotz, at a time like this?

LOTZ: At a time like this, it's almost easier to have faith, because we have nothing else. I've watched as this nation has turned to prayer. You know, we've seen the prayer vigils. I've watched the coverage of the prayer vigil in the Capitol last night. I think it's a time to turn to God. Those World Trade Center towers symbolize our nation. Our nation has been hit and devastated by this day of terror, and now I believe it's our choice as a nation as to whether we're going to implode and disintegrate emotionally and spiritually or whether we're going to make the choice to be stronger. Right now, we have the opportunity to come through this spiritually stronger than we've been in the past because we've turned to God.

CLAYSON: There's such a sense of anger among so many people and rightfully so. I've heard people say — those who are religious, those who are not — "If God is good, how could God let this happen?" To that, you say ...?

LOTZ: God is also angry when he sees something like this. And I would say also that for several years now, Americans, in a sense, have shaken their fists at God and said, "God, we want You out of the schools, we want You out of our government, we want You out of our business, we want You out of our marketplace." And God, who is a gentleman, has quietly backed out of our national and political life, our public life, removing His hand of blessing and protection. And we need to turn to God, first of all, and say, "God, we're sorry that we have treated You this way, and we invite You now to come into our national life. We put our trust in You." We have our *Trust in God* on our coins. We need to practice it.

CLAYSON: As a spiritual adviser, how would you define the feelings of so many people around this country right now?

LOTZ: I was watching television the first day, and they interviewed a construction worker who had been an eyewitness to all of this in a building next to the World Trade Center. And he said, "How do I feel?" He said, "I've seen planes hit this building. I've seen people falling out of the sky. My heart is in my throat." I feel like I would say the same thing. You don't have thoughts to articulate. Your heart is in your throat. You can hardly stand it. You're numb. But for myself, I fall back on my faith in God. Our foundation is faith in God, and the structure we build on that foundation is what enables us to endure something like this.

CLAYSON: You believe that even bringing these terrorists to justice won't bring complete peace for anyone. Why do you say that?

LOTZ: Not peace in the heart. There's nothing you can do that will bring your loved one back, nothing you can do that will put your life back the way it was before Tuesday. So finding the perpetrators is not going to comfort these people who have lost loved ones. That's a comfort only God can give. God knows what it's like to lose a loved one. He gave His only Son on the Cross, and He knows what it's like to stand by and see a loved one die a horrific death. So He understands, and He's emotionally involved in our pain, and He has the answers for us, and He can bring comfort that's beyond human understanding.

CLAYSON: There's such a feeling of helplessness among so many people here in New York and in Washington and around this country. What would be your recommendation as a spiritual adviser?

LOTZ: I thought Governor Keating said it well. When you asked him the first thing he did after the Oklahoma City bombing, he said pray. We need to pray, and we need to pray for people who can't pray for themselves right now. And I believe we need to call out to God and ask Him to forgive our sins and to heal our land. God is greater than sometimes we think of Him, and He can solve this. He can give us answers. He can give us wisdom. He can lead us through this in a way that makes us stronger as a nation, but we have to turn to Him.

CLAYSON: This event has changed our nation forever. What do you say about that?

LOTZ: I pray that God will use this event to change us forever in a positive way and to strengthen our faith in Him. I thought of all those people who have died in this tragedy, and it doesn't matter right now what political affiliation they had or what denomination they belonged to or what religion or what the color of their skin was or if they were old or young or their stock portfolio — what matters is their relationship with God. I would like to see Americans focus on the primary things — things that are more important than entertainment and pleasure and making more money.

CLAYSON: I'll let that be the last word. Mrs. Anne Graham Lotz, I appreciate seeing you this morning. Our best to your father, the Reverend Billy Graham.

LOTZ: Thank you, Jane, and I'll convey that to him. God bless you.

A transcript of the interview was captured on the Web and went around the globe as people emailed friends far and wide, sharing my words with a world that was looking for answers to the devastation resulting from the attack on America. By divine providence, Jeffrey Donaldson, a British member of Parliament from Belfast, Northern Ireland, received a forwarded copy of the transcript. After prayer and confirmation from other leaders, he extended to me an invitation to be the first person outside of Great Britain, and the first woman, to give the main address at the National Parliamentary Prayer Breakfast at Westminster Hall in London. I accepted.

The night before the prayer breakfast, a reception was held in the historic apartment of the Speaker of the House, the Right Honorable Michael Martin, MP, located inside the houses of Parliament. Mr. Donaldson shared with the several dozen specially invited political and religious leaders gathered that I had been invited to speak at the National Prayer Breakfast in the morning because he had read a transcript of the interview I had done on the CBS *Early Show*. He said he was convinced that what I had said in that interview was God's message for America after 9/11, and he was just as convinced God had given me a message for his nation. With a crackling fire on the hearth behind him, he turned toward me in that crowded room filled with dignitaries who were now hushed by his words and said, "We are praying that God will speak to us through you."

I returned to my hotel room and tore up the message I had so carefully prepared. In light of all that had transpired in the Speaker's apartment, it now seemed somehow insipid and canned. I fell on my knees and pleaded with God to honor Jeffrey Donaldson's courageous faith by giving me His message for the hour.

This book contains the message God gave to me that night as I trembled on my knees before Him. This is an expanded version of what I boldly delivered to more than six hundred national leaders in the same frigid hall where William Wallace, of *Braveheart* fame, had been executed and where the Queen Mother had lain in state.

This is a wake-up call to the church ... to the hearts of God's people. It is a call that ignites a longing to see Jesus again ...

A Longing to See Jesus . . . Again

M y schedule has been crazy for the last several months. Traveling, speaking, writing, and business matters coupled with home and family responsibilities have kept me so busy I've had no time for myself, much less time to drive the four hours west to visit my parents. In the few days when I might have pried back my schedule and squeezed in such a visit, I've had the flu — three times! My parents are struggling with their own health issues, so I don't dare come into their presence with even the slightest sniffle.

I have talked with my mother from time to time on the telephone. Such conversations always leave me uplifted; I love the sound of her voice. At the same time, when I hang up the phone I'm somewhat depressed because I'm not able to be with her in person — and I'm so aware she is not immortal.[1] I know I don't call her as much as I should or as much as I want to. I feel torn between where I am — here — and where I want to be — there, with her.

I long to see my mother . . . again. I long to sit beside the fire in her bedroom and see the sparkle in her dancing eyes as she relates some humorous anecdote. I long to see the intelligent expression on her beautiful, character-lined face as she listens to me share something with her. I long to see the welcoming gesture of her hands as she extends them to embrace me, or the quick gestures of her hands that spontaneously clap

with joy, or the elegant gestures of her hands as she toys absentmind-
edly with her pearl necklace, or the loving gentleness of her hands as
she strokes the well-worn pages of her Bible. I long to see her, I long to
hear her, I long to just be in her presence, because with all my heart, I
love my mother.

And as passionately as I love my mother and long to be with her,
I love Jesus even more. I talk with Him from time to time in prayer,
although I know I don't pray as much as I should or as much as I want
to. I love the sound of His voice when He speaks to me through His
Word. And I feel torn between where I am — here — and where I want
to be — there, with Him. I long for ...

the wind of His Spirit to breathe calmness into the chaos of my life.
the fullness of His wisdom to order the thoughts in my mind.
the sufficiency of His strength to undergird the weakness of my body.
the abundance of His blessing to saturate the poverty of my spirit.
the joy of His will to give rich pleasure to my journey.
the refuge of His arms to shield me from my fears.
the gentleness of His touch to reawaken the feelings of my heart.
the compassion of His heart to enfold me and hold me close.
I long to see Jesus ... again.

Considering how strong my love for Jesus is, you would expect my
hunger for His presence, my urgent longing to see Him again, to be a
constant, motivating force in my life. Yet sometimes, ...

in the busyness of my days

or the duties of my ministry

or the familiar habits of my worship

or the everyday routine of my home,

the longing becomes complacency, and I sleep through opportunities
to be with Him. That's when I most need a wake-up call — a jolt that
pushes me to seek out a revival of the passion that began as a blazing,

empowering fire but somehow tends to die down to a comfortable but weak, ineffective glow.

The revival I long for is not a tent meeting. It is not a series of church services designed to save the lost.

It is . . .

> "breathing the breath of God."
> "God purifying His church."
> "people saturated with God."
> "the inrush of the Spirit into a body that threatens to become a corpse."
> "a work of God's Spirit among His own people . . . what we call revival is simply New Testament Christianity, the saints getting back to normal."[2]

What is revival to you?

For some of us, the word *revival* provokes images of sawdust trails, emotional outbursts, off-key singing, finger-pointing preaching, and hell-fire praying. But the revival I'm talking about — the revival God is calling you and me to experience — is something completely different. It's authentic, *personal* revival.

A major, national newsmagazine recently ran a cover story on spirituality in America. The writer reported that spirituality, the impulse to communicate with the Divine, is thriving. The article stated that "75 percent of Americans say that a very important reason for their faith is to forge a personal relationship with God" and "that if you feel God within you, then the important question is settled. The rest is just details." The writer concluded that the world is filled with "hungry people, looking for a deeper relationship with God."[3]

Throughout this book, I'll do my best to explain how you can experience an authentic, deeper, richer relationship with God in a life-changing, fire-blazing revival. And interspersed along the way, I'll share with you the dramatic story of someone who has made personal revival a reality. Her name is Carole Inman; she is a real person, and I'm grateful that she is willing to let her story be used to help others. Carole begins by admitting, "Honestly, I didn't really even know what the word [revival] meant."

Yet on a dark, snowy night in Fargo, North Dakota, Carole experienced it for herself when she got a wake-up call and received a fresh encounter with Jesus that set her heart on fire for Him. As a result, she repented of her sin, returned to the Cross, and recommitted her life to serve Jesus Christ.

What Carole heard that night at a *Just Give Me Jesus* Revival kickoff was a message based on Isaiah's testimony recorded in the first six chapters of the Old Testament book that bears his name. It was the same message God had given me late that night before I was to address the breakfast gathering of members of Parliament the next morning. That message, which helped light a revival fire in Carole's heart — and I hope will ignite the same fire in yours — is contained in this book you now hold in your hands.

In these pages, rather than just define *revival*, I want to show you through Isaiah's testimony — and Carole's — what true, *personal* revival is. Like the old farmer who was showing his new farmhand around the barn ...

The farmer pointed out the stalls, the tack room, the feed bins, and the hay loft, then took the young man out back where his mule was kept. As he led the young man into the corral, the mule reared back and kicked the farmhand ten feet into the air. As the farmhand picked himself up off the ground, he shouted at the old man, "Why didn't you tell me the mule would kick like that?"

The old farmer leaned over, spat a long stream of tobacco over the fence, shifted the wad from one cheek to the other, than drawled, "Showin' is better 'n tellin'."

My prayer for you as you read this book is that the eyes of your heart will be opened and you will not just see what genuine revival is but that *you will see the Lord*.

Because personal revival is . . .

Jesus in you

and Jesus around you

and Jesus through you

and Jesus under you

and Jesus over you

and Jesus before you

and Jesus behind you.

Personal revival is *just Jesus* . . .

Jesus on your mind,

Jesus filling your heart,

Jesus overflowing from your lips.

So center down. Be still. Listen with the ears of your heart. Can you hear Him? The still, small voice of God is calling you to see Jesus . . . *again*. He is calling you to an experience of personal revival. Here. Now.

ONE

You're Sleeping!

Isaiah 1–5

You can know the right stuff in your head
but still be missing something.

Carole's Story

At the time the Lord dramatically changed the course of my Christian life, I wouldn't have characterized myself as someone needing "revival." Honestly, I didn't really even know what the word meant. Even my "church friends" probably wouldn't have labeled me as needing revival. Because, on the outside, my Christian walk looked like we're often told it should look. I had been a Christian for more than fifteen years. But, having accepted Christ as an adult, I could still vividly remember the time when I wasn't sure I would go to heaven if I died. And I certainly wasn't tired of giving thanks to God for the moment when He gave me assurance of my salvation.

I loved Him, and I was doing all I knew to do to live out my life in Christ. I . . .

. . . committed a time of personal devotion to the Lord each morning,

. . . attended a church that faithfully taught the Word of God,

. . . served in my church body as a deaconess, as a Sunday school teacher, by chairing our pastoral search committee, and by serving wherever else I was called upon,

. . . was part of a weekly cell group in my church, growing in God's Word,

. . . was in a weekly Bible study with other women,

*. . . surrounded myself with wonderful, godly friends who
    modeled Christ and challenged me, and . . .*

*. . . did my best to live out my faith in the marketplace, where I
    had been a corporate executive for twenty years.*

*That November, not only was I feeling blessed in my Christian
walk, I was feeling blessed by life in general. Feeling genuinely content in my singleness, I had a large, wonderful family that loved me,
complete with nieces and nephews who were a joy in my life. I had an
exciting job in the technology field that challenged and energized me.
I had the six-figure income that came with my business success, and
I was able to travel, live in a comfortable home, and buy whatever I
desired. I had my health and fitness that allowed me to run marathons, compete in triathlons, and to bike, ski, and enjoy just about
any other adventure someone would put before me.*

I loved the Lord. And I loved my life.

*If you would have asked me, I would have told you I was plenty
alive . . .*

~:~

Hey! You've Missed Something

Surrounded by lines of patience-ready-to-snap passengers, luggage
grouped at my feet like overweight sentinels signaling an international
trip, my eyes were focused intently on the agent behind the desk. While
I silently urged the passenger in front of me to hurry up, I felt a gentle,
friendly tap on my shoulder. When I turned, I saw a face wreathed in
smiles belonging to a good friend. After giving him a hug, I asked what
he was doing in line. As he described the international adventure that

was before him, I had a very difficult time maintaining an interested, straight face because I was acutely aware that his belt was undone and his fly was open! He'd obviously missed something very important, and he didn't even know it! I'm sorry to say that I wasn't a very good friend — my embarrassment for him kept me from saying anything to him. I have wondered how far he got on his journey before someone pointed out, "Hey! Wake up! You've missed something!"

I have also wondered how many Christians, like my friend, are missing something very important and don't know it, either. Something that one day may be cause, not for embarrassment, but for shame. While my friend was missing something very basic and obvious — zipping his pants and buckling his belt — could it be that you as a Christian are missing something just as basic and obvious? And I am left to wonder how far you will get on your journey of faith before you realize, *Something's missing.* Would you allow me the privilege of being your friend and telling you what it is? What's missing is knowing God ... *with your heart!*

For years, Tom Landry was an American icon. With the brim of his hat pulled down over a stoic face, he paced the sidelines of football fields where he presided as head coach over one of the greatest teams of all time, the Dallas Cowboys. He faced pressure with poise, criticism with grace, rudeness with courtesy, humiliation with dignity, victory with humility, and crisis with faith. He became a legend in his own time.

On more than one occasion, I have heard Coach Landry state that during his career he came across many good athletes — but very few great ones. He said the difference between a good athlete and a great one is eighteen inches — the distance from the head to the heart. From his observation based on a lifetime of involvement in sports, he explained that good athletes have exceptional ability and a thorough understanding of the game, but great athletes have heart — a passion to play that drives them to selfless sacrifice, brutally long hours of practice, undivided focus, and ultimately, to achieve extraordinary accomplishments.

In almost thirty years of ministry, I have observed many good Christians, like Coach Landry's athletes, but very few great ones. And the difference is the same eighteen inches — the distance from the head to the heart. While there are many good Christians who have a head knowledge of Scripture, attend church regularly, are familiar with church traditions and rituals, and are comfortable with prayer, group Bible study, and outreach ministries, there are very few who are great.

There are relatively few Christians who are in love with Jesus, who put Him first in their lives when doing so demands that they sacrifice their own time, money, and desires. There are very few Christians who want what He wants more than what they want — and are willing to lay everything on the line to pursue it. There are very few Christians who are willing to risk their job, reputation, status, friendships, financial security, and even their life for the sake of sharing the gospel and pleasing God. We just seem to lack a clear knowledge of God and a passionate heart for God that, combined, are the hub around which everything in our life should revolve.

Not only do some of us who call ourselves Christians lack heart knowledge of God, we don't even seem to have much head knowledge either. We know God's name and job description — isn't He the One who lives in heaven and sends people to hell? We know Jesus died on the Cross to save us, but we're really not sure from what, although we have prayed and asked Him to come into our heart. And we know going to church is the right thing to do and makes us feel good. Besides, we can make nice friends and develop strategic business contacts there. And spiritual gifts? Aren't they what we exchange at Christmas?

If we're honest, even though we're authentic Christians, we would say that although we don't know much, the little we do know is more *about God* then actually *knowing God* Himself.

Others of us have exceptional gifts that we exercise in an endless variety of church activities. We seem to have a working knowledge of God in our heads —

we can quote Scripture ...

we can pray out loud ...

we can sing many hymns from memory ...

we can list some of God's names with their meanings ...

we can give a vague account of creation ...

we can give a thumbnail sketch of the history of Israel ...

we can define names like Abraham, Moses, David, and Elijah ...

we can dramatize the birth, death, and resurrection of Jesus ...

we can trace the three journeys of Paul

(with help from the maps) ...

we avoid the Holy Spirit and the book of Revelation ...

— and we seem to be satisfied that that's that!

Why is it that we, and so many others who call themselves by God's name, seem to lack heart ...

for His Word?

for prayer?

for the gospel of Jesus Christ?

for a lost and dying world?

for each other?

for Him?

Our selfish attitudes and ambitions demand to know what's in it for us ...

> before we sacrifice anything,
> before we give time (if it's convenient),
> before we give money (if there's some left over),
> before we tear away our all-consuming focus from ourselves,
>> our families and our friends,
>> our concerns and our careers,
>> our struggles and our status,
>> our pleasures and our possessions,
>> our bank accounts and our stock portfolios,
>> our exercise and our entertainment,
>> our debts and our diets,

and from just about anything else other than the kingdom of God. Why is it that we can be passionate about our favorite sports team, or a job promotion, or a dreamed-of vacation spot, or our alma mater, or a weekly televised reality show, or even the latest weight-loss plan, *but we don't have that same passion about the things of God?*

I believe the answer is that there is more to knowing God than just head knowledge alone.

I believe the kingdom of God is desperate for churches that are filled, not with good Christians, but filled with great ones — Christians whose knowledge of God has made the eighteen-inch drop from their heads to their hearts.

Until that drop occurs within us, we lack heart because we lack vision.

I believe we are living in a generation that *desperately needs a fresh vision of God.* We are living in a precarious worldwide situation where terrorism and war take center stage and where God is being pushed to the perimeter of our cultural and personal life — just at the time when we need Him most. As if to underscore this, less than three weeks after Hurricane Katrina destroyed so many lives, a California district judge decided the Pledge of Allegiance was unconstitutional because it included the phrase "under God."[1] History shows us what can happen when a civilization turns its back on God — and it also shows us the extraordinary changes that can happen when a fresh knowledge of God is sought after and reincorporated into a culture's priorities. This contrast is dramatically illustrated in the life of Isaiah during the Old Testament days ...

Isaiah was a prophet in Judah[2] during a period that followed approximately fifty-two years of peace and prosperity. Although nearby nations boiled in turmoil, Judah was mostly free of unrest. But instead of using those years of peace and prosperity to grow strong, the people of Judah had drifted so far from God that they teetered on the brink of moral and spiritual bankruptcy. Their disobedience to His Word ... their disregard of His precepts ... their defiance of His law ... were provoking His judgment.

At this critical time in Judah's history, in the year 741 BC, when Judah as a nation was sliding into judgment, God raised up a man who became the most outstanding of the Old Testament prophets. What ...

Shakespeare is to literature,

and Beethoven is to music,

and Michelangelo is to art,

Isaiah is to prophecy.

He is simply the greatest. But he didn't become great until the year King Uzziah died. That was the time when Isaiah's head knowledge of God dropped eighteen inches to his heart. It was the pivotal, life-changing year when Isaiah experienced a wake-up call that opened his eyes to a fresh vision of God. It was the unforgettable moment when he exclaimed, "I saw the LORD!"

Those of us who are living in the Western Hemisphere have also experienced approximately half a century of relative peace and prosperity, while much of the world has been in turmoil. Like Judah, we believe God's past blessings are an indication He will keep us safe. We have not used this period to grow morally and spiritually strong. Instead we have become arrogant in our disregard for God, trusting in His blessings instead of in Him, and therefore we are so weakened in our relationship with God that we too may be provoking His judgment.

May God help us, as He helped Judah, by raising up men and women who speak forth His Word with the power to change lives — a power that is rooted in their own personal *vision* of the Lord. My prayer is that this book might be a wake-up call to *you,* who, by following Isaiah's example and being ignited by God's Spirit, will have your own eyes opened to a fresh vision of the Lord. And I pray that as your life is impacted, it, in turn, will be a life that is empowered to change the lives of others. But first . . .

You Think You're Okay

If you think you don't need personal revival — that your life is fine the way it is . . . Or if you think you're not qualified — not devout enough or wise enough or even brave enough to experience this kind of powerful, personal, life-changing revival — you have lots of company. I've felt the same way.

And I suspect Isaiah did too — right up until that moment when he experienced his own wake-up call and his knowledge of God dropped from his head to his heart. There is no inkling in Scripture that Isaiah felt he needed personal revival. There is not a shred of biblical evidence that indicates he had any awareness of need in his life. He thought he was okay. Yet when he heard the wake-up call and experienced revival, his life was never the same, and he became someone God used to powerfully impact his generation. By his own example, he teaches us that prophets need revival too, whether or not they realize it.

Come along with me and examine the life of Israel's greatest prophet as he shares his testimony in Isaiah 1 – 6. As we begin our journey along the pathway Isaiah followed, in this section we'll look at Isaiah's life *before* he got his spiritual wake-up call. You may be surprised to find some characteristics of your own sleeping heart in Isaiah's descriptions.

You've Never Had a Vision (and You Aren't Sure You Want One)

The word *vision* makes me think of Ebenezer Scrooge and the ghosts of Christmas past, present, and future. It makes me think of a medium hunched over a crystal ball, zoned out in a trance, or of ghostly apparitions, or of things some televangelists use to demand that I send them money. A vision can seem so, well, mystical ... spooky ... weird ... unreal ... and yes, even manipulative. I'm not sure I want one!

I doubt that Isaiah himself wanted a vision, especially the kind I just described. The Bible gives no indication that Isaiah felt he needed personal revival or had any awareness whatsoever of any spiritual deficiencies at all. Nevertheless, when the wake-up call came, the vision he saw was nothing like those cited above. Instead it catapulted his spirit into the center of the universe — into the very throne room of heaven.

It gave him keen insight into the heart of God.

It riveted his focus on the Son of God.

It flooded him with fresh hope for himself and his beloved people.

It unveiled the thrilling, awesome glory of Jesus Christ.

It was a forceful experience that propelled Isaiah into personal revival that lasted a lifetime.

And once he had that vision, he must have wondered how he could ever have lived without it. But *before* the vision, he seemed comfortable with who he was.

Today, as in the year 741 BC, God is longing for those who think they're okay — who feel secure in their moral and religious foundation — to wake up.[3] Wake up to Him!

You're Secure in Your Moral and Religious Foundation

My father has always been keenly interested in world affairs. Even now, editions of international, national, and local newspapers are delivered to my father each day. He subscribes to all the major newsmagazines and reads them thoroughly. In the evening, invariably as supper is about to be placed on the table, my father stops all activity and watches the evening network news on television. While he can converse with great interest about the weather or my mother's latest purchase or a neighbor's family, his conversation and even his prayers are peppered with his conscious awareness of what is taking place in the world around him. He has a passionate worldview that has kept him on the sharp edge of commitment in his service to God.

Because of my father's example in the home, I was raised with an awareness that the world is bigger than my immediate circle of friends, family, church, school, community, and career. It is almost instinctive for me to feel some personal responsibility to do something about the problems I see.

It seems that Isaiah was also raised in a good home. He lived in Judah and served God "during the reigns of Uzziah, Jotham, Ahaz and Hezekiah" (Isaiah 1:1), as well as during the reign of the wicked Manasseh, when the culture as Isaiah had known it totally disintegrated around him.[4] Yet in the midst of a collapsing culture, Isaiah's personal foundation of moral values and faith in God seems to have been established early in his home.

Little is known of Isaiah's background except that he was "the son of Amoz" (1:1). I've wondered if Amoz was a man who cared deeply about those around him, teaching his young son by his own example to care ...

> about world events
>> and national trends
>>> and local problems
>>>> and political change
>>>>> and moral decay
>>>>>> and a neighbor's need.

I wonder if Amoz was someone like my own father.

In what kind of home were you raised? Was it a home like Isaiah's? Or was it a home where there was no faith in God at all, and no moral values were ever imparted? Was it a home that was very self-centered? If so, then you may have seen up close and personal the genuine need for people to be awakened in their relationship to God — for their hearts to be enlarged to love Him and to love others as they love themselves. But you may have worked so intently to help them with their needs (and shortcomings) that you have overlooked your own.

You're Focused on "Them"

Being aware of the needs of others, whether in the world at large or within our own homes, is a truly Christlike perspective. Yet sometimes we can become so fixated on the problems in our world and in the lives of those around us that we are blinded to things that are wrong in our own lives. We can become so focused on others that we don't see ourselves. If we aren't careful — if we don't have a clear vision of God — we may slip into self-righteousness and judgmentalness and spiritual pride and condemnation.

Before his wake-up call, Isaiah was someone who was consumed with what was wrong with "them." Whether or not it was because of the example Amoz set in the home, Isaiah was someone who had a deep sense of moral and spiritual responsibility to get involved in his world. He was keenly aware of the problems his people faced:

poverty,[5]

oppression of the poor,[6]

indifference to the weak,[7]

government corruption,[8]

religious hypocrisy.[9]

Their Primary Problem

Like Isaiah, even a casual observer of our world today can list many problems ...

deals behind closed doors,

whispers behind backs,

agendas hidden in political posturing,

abuse of power that's portrayed as political savvy,

spin doctors that misinform the public,

destruction of the environment,

preoccupation with perverted pleasure,

exploitation of the human body,

abuse of innocent children,

spoiled goods sold as fresh,

dangerous chemicals labeled safe,

covenants broken by a whim,

truth exchanged for lies,

glory given to the obnoxious,

honor given to the blasphemous,

legalized acceptance of abomination.

While each of these problems is a major challenge in itself, you and I need to acknowledge what Isaiah acknowledged — that there was a common denominator. The primary problem Judah faced in Isaiah's day is exactly the same primary problem we are facing today. The . . .

> primary
> fundamental
> basic
> bottom-line
> problem . . .
> . . . *is sin!*

Sin is what's wrong in our world today! And it was what was wrong in Isaiah's day as well. So Isaiah, who cared deeply about the problems his world was immersed in, pinpointed their root cause when he mourned, "Ah, sinful nation, a people loaded with guilt, a brood of evildoers, children given to corruption! They have forsaken the Lord; they have spurned the Holy One of Israel and turned their backs on him" (1:4).

Judah had been founded on faith in God, but as Isaiah began his ministry he observed that God's people were forsaking Him. As the people "spurned the Holy One of Israel and turned her back on him" did they cover up their sin by labeling it separation of church and state? Or tolerance of other religions?

Isaiah's words were strong, unvarnished, cutting, and totally intolerant of such national sin. He bluntly called sin the way he saw it. And, more importantly, because he was a prophet of God, we would assume he called sin the way *God* saw it.

I wonder what words he would use today to describe our nation that also was founded on faith in God yet now seems to be rewriting history in order to reject any relationship with Him . . .

Like an arrow finding the bull's-eye of a target, Isaiah's words have an even more solemn meaning that strikes much closer to home when we realize he was speaking to Judah — *God's people* — who were identified with God's name.

Today, God's people, who are called by His name, are professing Christians. You and I. People within the church. Today, could a legitimate paraphrase of Isaiah's prophetic condemnation be something like this …?

Ah, sinful church, a people loaded with guilt because while you have a form of godliness you deny the power of the Cross alone to cleanse and transform and radically change lives.[10] You are a brood of evildoers who call on Jesus as Lord and speak His Word and do many good works yet have never established a personal relationship with God through faith in Jesus Christ.[11] You are children given to corruption because you have conformed to the pattern of the world around you instead of separating yourselves from it.[12] You — the church — have forsaken the Lord. You — the Bride — have spurned the Holy One — your Bridegroom — and have turned your back on Him.

Strong words. But are they strong enough today for the organized church whose leadership preys on innocent children, sexually abusing them, then covers up the sin and allows the perpetrators to continue in ministry?! Are they strong enough for the church that closes its doors to people of a different race or different socioeconomic background?! Are they strong enough for the church that officially sanctions abomination by ordaining practicing homosexuals into the ministry — or marrying them?! Are they strong enough for the church that supports missions in Africa but steps over the homeless lying at their front door! I wonder … *What words would Isaiah have used for the organized church today?*

Not too long before writing this, I spoke at a citywide meeting that had been organized by one of our teams in preparation for *Just Give Me Jesus,* a revival for women that is jointly sponsored by a group of local leaders and my ministry organization, AnGeL Ministries. The audience was made up of Christian leaders from throughout the surrounding area who had come for information and inspiration. Dozens of churches had sent representatives. The historic downtown venue where the meeting was held crackled with anticipation as hundreds of people prayed together and sang together and listened attentively as I conveyed the vision God had given me for the revival of the hearts of His people in that area.

Immediately behind me as I stood giving the message was a choir from a mainline church in the city that had led us in worship earlier. About ten minutes into my message, I heard a crash behind me, then the loud footsteps of someone stomping off the stage. I kept my concentration on what I was saying and continued with the message. In a few moments, I heard the muffled sound of movement coming from the same area. Not wanting to allow the message or the meeting to be unduly distracted, I continued without interruption. My assumption was that the choir seated behind me had decided to relocate because they wanted more of a frontal view or because the members had found it difficult to hear, which is often the case for those seated on stage if the monitors are not arranged properly.

When I finished the message and returned to my front-row seat, to my astonishment, I saw that the choir that stood to perform the closing song had only half of the original two dozen members. It was only later that I learned that the choir had staged a walkout in protest of my brief reference to a specific sin! A few days later they took their protest to the front pages of the newspaper accusing *me* of preaching hate and intolerance!

When I was asked what I thought about the incident, I responded by saying it underscored the need for the revival ministry to which God has called me and the crying need for repentance from sin — within the church!

Their Primary Solution

Isaiah clearly understood that the primary problem in Judah was sin — and sin is also the primary problem in our world today. And if sin is the primary problem, then the primary solution is not medical, environmental, educational, economical, social, racial, or political. If the primary problem, in our world and in Isaiah's, is (and was) sin, then the primary solution is a Savior who will take away that sin and make people right with God.

Isaiah pled with God's people to repent, quoting God Himself: "'Come now, let us reason together,' says the LORD. 'Though your sins are like scarlet, they shall be as white as snow; though they are red as crimson, they shall be like wool'" (1:18). The invitation Isaiah issued was the equivalent of an Old Testament presentation of the gospel, inviting people to the Cross. He knew that God's people needed to be deeply, thoroughly, completely cleansed of their sin.

Isaiah's plea can be heard in God's promise given earlier to King Solomon and quoted frequently today in church pulpits and Sunday school classrooms and seminary lecture halls and private conversations and around kitchen tables: "When I shut up the heavens so that there is no rain, or command locusts to devour the land or send a plague among my people, if my people, who are called by my name, will humble themselves and pray and seek my face and turn from their wicked ways, then will I hear from heaven and will forgive their sin and will heal their land."[13]

As we thoughtfully consider God's promise to King Solomon, the phrase-by-phrase application to our own world is extremely relevant:

"When I shut up the heavens so that there is no rain…"

When there are record-breaking…

snowstorms,

and floods,

and forest fires,

and droughts,

and hurricanes,

and tornadoes,

and tsunamis…

"or command locusts to devour the land…"

an accidental release of killer bees,

an invasion of fire ants,

another occurrence of hoof-and-mouth

or mad cow disease…

"or send a plague among my people…"

AIDS,

SARS,

STDs,

West Nile virus,

bird flu…

"if my people, who are called by my name, will humble themselves and pray and seek my face and turn from their wicked ways, then will I hear from heaven and will forgive their sin and will heal their land."[14]

Even as Americans say and pray and sing "God Bless America," it would appear that His blessing on a nation is directly related to the church — God's people, who are called by His name — waking up and getting right with God.

After the horrific devastation of 9/11, many church leaders were pointing their fingers at national or social sins as the reason for what they saw as God's judgment on our nation. Abortion on demand and the broad acceptance of homosexuality were the grievous sins most commonly noted. But I couldn't help wondering if the Son of God was focused on His own people, the church, with eyes "like blazing fire and … feet … like burnished bronze."[15] While I know the attack on America was a plot hatched in hell and carried out by wicked, evil minions of the devil, I am equally convinced it was allowed by God as a wake-up call to His people.

To me. *To you.*[16]

Maybe the church was listening …

Because in the aftermath of Hurricane Katrina, there was a lot of finger-pointing at virtually every level of our society — by government officials as well as ordinary citizens. Frustration reached the boiling point as relief and rescue seemed *soooo* slow in arriving. But again and again, heartwarming stories emerged of churches that opened their doors and hearts and homes, making God's resources available to those who so desperately needed them. All over the country, Christians rose up and responded by embracing the victims in a beautiful demonstration of God's love.

Yet the underlying message of impending judgment, and the need to prepare today for what may happen tomorrow, seemed to fall on deaf ears. The message that seemed to be written in the filthy, flooded streets of a major American city that had become a ghost town almost overnight, was, "Repent of your sin. Judgment is coming. Get right with God."

But the message seemed to be muffled by angry voices blaming everyone and anyone for the devastation. Voices that politicized something that was a God-sized problem and needed a God-given solution. Voices that seemed to dominate and drown out those few brave souls who courageously gave testimony to God's presence and protection in the midst of the disaster and who urged fellow sufferers to call on Him for help and hope.

Glued to the television newscasts following the hurricane, I watched as an obviously poor African-American woman was interviewed. She was trying to make her way into the Superdome, hoping to find shelter, food, and water. When the interviewer asked her what she thought of all she had been through, she said clearly and firmly, "God's tellin' us we need to repent of our sin."

I wonder ... how many people who heard what she had to say on the nightly news didn't truly "listen" to her message? I expect it would be safe to assume that the majority of viewers that night just didn't get it.

Like you and me, Isaiah lived in a world that didn't listen and therefore just didn't get God's message, either. Again and again, God warned His people of impending judgment if they refused to repent of their sin and get right with Him. Isaiah was committed to preaching God's Word in an effort to convict God's people of their sin — a conviction that would lead to repentance, restoration, and a stay of judgment.

Living in a world that is similar to Isaiah's in many respects — a world that is rapidly changing in almost every area — I am committed to the unchanging Word of God for the same reason Isaiah was committed to it.

You're Committed to God's Word

Our world is changing more rapidly than most of us comprehend ...
   scientific discoveries,
      technological advances,
         medical breakthroughs,
            communication speed,
               economic fluctuation,
                  moral disintegration,
                the realignment of nations,
            shifting political alliances,
       Third World powers with first world weapons,
all help to create an impression of ...
   a world that is ruled by chance,
      a world that is geared for the young and energetic,
         a world that is spinning out of control,
            a world that no longer makes sense,
               a world of exciting opportunities,
                  a world of frightening possibilities,
                     a world that is in dire need of stability.

In order to have lasting peace and security, our world needs to be anchored to a foundation that never changes. King David praised God, declaring, "Your word, O LORD, is eternal; it stands firm in the heavens."[17] Jesus Himself underscored the stability of the unchanging Word of God when He testified, "I tell you the truth, until heaven and earth disappear, not the smallest letter, not the least stroke of a pen, will by any means disappear from the Law until everything is accomplished."[18]

A changing world needs the Word of God to stabilize it. You and I, living in a changing world, need the Word of God to stabilize us! We need God's wisdom and guidance and comfort and hope that He offers to us through His Word. And we need to be in a right relationship with Him in order to not only survive the rapid changes and challenges but to seize the opportunities to make our changing world a better place.

If our world *is* to be a better place, we have to deal with the primary problem we face:

Sin. In our own hearts and lives.

Isaiah knew that solving Judah's primary problem required convicting God's people of their sin so they would seek to be made right with God. He was committed to God's Word because it is like a schoolmaster: it teaches people that they are sinners, and it tells them about the Savior.[19]

For two years Isaiah preached God's Word:

"Hear, O heavens! Listen, O earth! *For the* Lord *has spoken.*"[20]

"Hear the *word of the* Lord."[21]

"Listen to *the law of our God.*"[22]

"'The multitude of your sacrifices — what are they to me?' *says the* Lord."[23]

"'Come now, let us reason together,' *says the* Lord."[24]

"For the mouth of *the* Lord *has spoken.*"[25]

"Therefore the Lord, the Lord Almighty, *the Mighty One of Israel, declares. ...*"[26]

Isaiah preached God's Word. He did not substitute anything at all for eternal truth and divine revelation. He did not apologize for preaching the straight, pure, unadulterated Word of God. He did not compromise or water it down to make it less offensive. He did not dress it up to make it more attractive.

Today, we seem to have a variety of substitutes for straight, plain Bible preaching. We seem to depend more on ...

audios or videos,

musicals or formulas,

social issues or political agendas,

denominational materials or religious rituals,

even books about God's Word ...

until the average church member is biblically illiterate! But there is no substitute for God's Word.

It's the Word that cuts through the political correctness of our day, exalting Jesus Christ as "the way and the truth and the life."[27]

It's the Word that confronts all the religious systems of the world and plainly states that "no one comes to the Father except through me [Jesus]."[28]

It's the Word that rebukes the atheist and evolutionist by flatly stating that "in the beginning God created the heavens and the earth."[29]

It's the Word that humbles the philanthropist by rejecting any and all charity as a basis for salvation, because "all of us have become like one who is unclean, and all our righteous acts are like filthy rags."[30]

It's the Word that sets straight the self-righteous moralists who believe their good deeds will outweigh their bad deeds and God will owe them a heavenly home when it clarifies, "There is no one righteous, not even one."[31]

It's the Word that convicts us of our sin,

and *it's the Word* that tells us we need a Savior,

and *it's the Word* that proclaims:

"Salvation is found in no one else, for there is no other name under heaven given to men by which we must be saved."[32]

It's the Word that gives us a glimpse into the very heart of God for our changing world when it reveals, "For God so loved the world that he gave his one and only Son, that whoever believes in him shall not perish but have eternal life."[33]

Praise God for His Word! Praise God for prophets like Isaiah who faithfully proclaimed it in the past! Praise God for men and women today in the pulpits of churches, in the lecterns of Sunday schools, in the fellowship of Bible studies, and in the classrooms of seminaries who live in a changing world and are absolutely committed to proclaiming the unchanging Word of God!

You're Unaware That Something's Still Missing

Isaiah passionately strived to make God's people aware of His call to them; he urged them to repent of their sin and to get right with their Creator. Like Carole, he was completely devoted to his God and to serving God's people. So it's understandable that Isaiah seemed unaware that he lacked anything spiritually. There is no biblical evidence to suggest that he perceived any such need at all. In fact, there is much to indicate the opposite — that he believed his relationship with God was right and strong and the basis for a powerful prophetic ministry in Judah. His preaching exuded confidence in who God is and in what God had said and in the need for His people to get right with Him. There is no indication that Isaiah was aware of his own need to make the eighteen-inch plunge from his head to his heart.[34]

And yet ...

Before Isaiah saw the Lord, his understanding of the changing world and his commitment to the Word of God seemed for the most part to be head knowledge. He intellectually grasped that the root cause of the world's problems was sin, he mentally believed that the solution was a Savior who would take away the sin and restore humankind in a right relationship with God, and he was right on target. But as he ardently toiled on God's behalf, Isaiah was missing something. He was unaware that God wanted Isaiah's knowledge of Him to drop eighteen inches — from his head to his heart.

Do you sometimes look at other Christians whose faith seems so vibrantly alive and wonder what they have that you don't? Are you somewhat resentful of the way they speak so personally about God, as though they actually know Him intimately? Deep down within, do you yearn for more in your relationship with Him, yet you don't know how to get it or even what to ask for? You know God — and yet *you know something's missing!*

In order to find what's missing...

in order for your desire for something more to deepen into an experience...

in order for your knowledge of God to drop the eighteen inches from your head to your heart...

you need personal revival.

And personal revival is something that is impossible for you to do on your own because it involves a quiet, miraculous, eye-opening revelation of Him within your spirit. So...

you need a vision.

You need to see the Lord. And to see the Lord requires an act of God...

you need His help.

And His help often goes unrecognized because it seems unrelated to your desire to draw near to Him in an intimate relationship. In fact, it may seem like the antithesis of receiving the fullness of His blessing. Because often it doesn't appear at first as a vision. Many times it comes disguised as a problem or pressure or stress or suffering or crisis... because first, God has to wake up our sleeping hearts.

TWO

Wake Up!

Isaiah 6:1

Storms can be God's messengers.

Carole's Story

I experienced significant testing in the twelve months leading up to my personal revival that I now can look back and see was preparation . . .

A tumor was discovered that required a hysterectomy. Still in my thirties at the time, it wasn't just a medical blow, it was also the end to any visions I may have had of a family of my own.

No sooner had I recovered from that surgery when, a month later, I was rushed into the hospital with a severe case of pancreatitis, brought on by a diseased gall bladder. I had gone from being a picture of health to having my second lengthy hospital stay in a two-month period.

Just when things seemed to be getting back to normal, a freak June rainstorm flooded the lower level of my home with sewer water, ruining every belonging it touched and setting off a seemingly endless round of meetings with insurance adjusters, contractors, and construction workers. All this was happening in the middle of an intensely busy time at work.

The calamities seemed to travel in pairs. A few weeks later, the Fourth of July brought a freak windstorm that blew the corner off the roof of my home.

Underlying that entire yearlong period, one of the most important friendships in my life was strained to such a point I wasn't certain it would survive. That situation, alone, would have made the year one of the lowest in my life.

In less than twelve months, I had seen my health fail, my property damaged, a close friendship threatened — all while my workload at the office escalated . . .

⋌∴⋋

His Message Is Not in a Bottle, It's in the Storm

Carole's story vividly illustrates how life-shaking experiences can prepare us for a fresh encounter with God.

Today as . . .

> financial empires come and go,
>> nations rise and fall,
>>> treaties are made and broken,
>>>> fortunes are accumulated and lost,
>>>> weather patterns defy all reason, and
>>>>> wars and rumors of wars rage all over the globe . . .

could it be that, from God's vantage point, *nothing* is more important than an experience of personal revival?

For many of us, our first connection with God comes as we're led to Him as children by our parents. Or it happens when an inspiring gospel service pulls us up out of our seat and sends us stumbling to the front of the church to publicly accept Jesus as our Lord and Savior. But in time, our passion wanes, and our connection to God remains locked in our heads without making that move into our hearts. Then something happens: some sort of setback — or multiple setbacks, as Carole endured. We automatically feel attacked, and we don't understand why such "bad luck" is happening to us. But in those moments of despair, remember that God has *allowed* the crisis, and you and I need to be watchful for His message within the life-storm. It just might be our wake-up call. It just might be that our experience of personal revival will be triggered by a vision of the Lord that is ushered in, not in a serene moment or a religious setting, but through a life-shaking event.

Whenever something catastrophic takes place internationally, as occurred when the deadly tsunami struck South Asia, or nationally, as happened when terrorists struck America on 9/11, or when Hurricane Katrina roared ashore in 2005, or when deadly bombs explode as they did in London, Madrid, and Bali, or when catastrophe strikes us personally in a diagnosis of disease or some kind of family disaster, you and I need to develop the habit of asking God what message there might be in it.

This concept of a storm containing a message from God is clearly illustrated in the life of another Old Testament prophet, Ezekiel. Ezekiel had been taken captive by King Nebuchadnezzar of Babylon, then discarded to live in a refugee camp. While sitting beside a dirty irrigation canal in Babylon, Ezekiel related that, "I looked, and I saw a windstorm coming out of the north — an immense cloud with flashing lightning and surrounded by brilliant light. . . . And in the fire was what looked like four living creatures."[1] His testimony goes on to describe the unique message from God that was brought to him on the wings of that storm.

Without question, the attack on America on September 11, 2001, was a storm that had international, national, and personal impact. I believe contained in that storm were messages from God, one of which was for the church in America. The message seemed loud and clear: *It's time to get serious about your relationship with God, about a lost and dying world that's going to hell apart from faith in Christ, about the gospel, and about the hope of heaven and eternal life.*

I truly believe that was God's message in the storm. But I don't think God's people, generally speaking, got it. Not yet — because our hearts are asleep. Sometimes we need to be shaken awake.

Shaken Awake by a Mortal Storm

Have you ever been present when someone actually stepped into eternity? One such occasion that comes to my mind was when I went to the hospital to visit one of my dearest friends, who was holding a death-bed vigil for her ninety-five-year-old father-in-law. The room was small and sterile. The hospital bed in the center of the room was occupied by a tall, thin man whose most obvious characteristics were his ashen gray coloring and his slightly rattled breathing.

My friend was by his side, where she had been for hours, accompanied by her sister-in-law, the dying man's daughter. When I entered the room, both women rose to their feet, embraced me, and stood to visit briefly. Their backs were to the bed as they faced me, so that I could see them and at the same time see the elderly gentleman lying on the bed behind them.

As we talked, I was aware of the old man breathing peacefully, then shuddering quietly for a moment before he lay perfectly still. Gently, I told my friend, "I think Mr. George has just entered heaven." And he had. As my friend and her sister-in-law held hands with me, I prayed, thanking God for the man's life, for his family, and now for his peaceful exit from this life into the next.

When I left the hospital, I was struck by how simply and how quickly death had come. One moment Mr. George had been alive, and the next moment he was in heaven. And I thought to myself, *Eternity is just a breath away!*

In the year 739 BC, King Uzziah died. His passing is a small footnote in the history of the world, and yet it seemed at the time to be the life-shaking experience that ushered Isaiah into his vision of the Lord. And it was that vision of the glory of the Lord that triggered Isaiah's personal revival.

It's worth noting that 739 BC was also the year that the city of Rome was initially founded, and subsequently, the Roman Empire. And it's interesting to see that while the Bible makes no mention of such a momentous event in the world of nations it does devote an entire chapter to describing one man's experience of personal revival. The conclusion is that one person waking up in his relationship to God, making the eighteen-inch transition from his head to his heart, is more important, from God's perspective, than an entire world empire being established.

Isaiah's writings indicate he may have lived in the king's palace.[2] So I wonder . . . how was Isaiah given the news of King Uzziah's death? Was he sitting in his luxurious apartment within the king's palace, working diligently on his next sermon, his heart passionately on fire to preach the truth of God's Word to "them"? Was he thanking God, even as he pored over the Scriptures, for giving him such clear insight into the primary problem and the primary solution for his people? Was he strategizing his next opportunity to preach so that it would have maximum impact? Then did he suddenly hear the clattering of sandals running on the slick surface of the marble hall and seconds later find himself startled by one of the king's aides, who burst through the heavily draped entrance to his chambers, fell on his knees, and reported, with tears streaming down his cheeks, "The king is dead!"

I wonder if Isaiah spontaneously jumped up out of his chair and exclaimed, "No! No! No! It can't be! That can't be right! I just saw the king last week! I was just thinking about visiting him tonight! How could he be dead?"

The suddenness of the tragedy must have made his world stop. I will never forget where I was and what I was doing when I heard the news that President John F. Kennedy had been shot. The effect of that news was a sudden, startling cessation of any and all routine activity as not just my world but literally the entire world was plunged into immediate horror and grief.

And I wonder, when Isaiah stood at the tomb and saw Uzziah buried, was he struck suddenly with the brevity and the finality of life? As he looked at the lifeless form of the king, was he shaken personally with the thought that *life must be about more than living?* Did he ask himself what in his own life would last beyond the grave? What was he doing that had eternal significance?

I will also never forget standing in the pulpit of a packed and overflowing church, looking down on the rose-draped coffin of one of my closest friends who had died suddenly from a deadly virus. Even as I delivered the funeral homily, I was shaken by the *temporariness of life.* One moment my friend had been healthy, vibrant, laughing, cooking, gardening, sewing, decorating, planning, loving — and twenty-four hours later she was in eternity! That was a life-shaking experience for me! I stepped out of the pulpit more committed than ever to live a life that would keep on living — *even after my death* — through the changed lives resulting from my faithful obedience to God's call in my life.

Because my limited experience with death has given me a keen sense of my own mortality, I would assume Isaiah was also shaken in the same way.

And my experience with death has also shaken me emotionally.

Shaken Awake by an Emotional Storm

In 2005 our world was flooded with pictures of human grief and despair following the devastating tsunami in South Asia. We watched in horror as our television screens brought into our living rooms the contorted faces of mothers who had had their infants snatched out of their arms; the inconsolable victims whose entire families were wiped out without a trace; the horrified, glazed eyes of health officials peering out above air-filtering masks as they stared numbly at dead bodies draped over tree limbs, washed up on beaches, and stacked like cordwood in temples.

> Villages vanished,
> businesses erased,
> lives destroyed,
> topography altered,
> hope evaporated.

And everywhere there was, and will be for a long time, unbearable grief. "Everything is broken, everyone is crying!" was the heartfelt testimony of one Sri Lankan.[3]

I wonder if everyone in Isaiah's world was crying, too. According to tradition, there is a slight chance that King Uzziah was a relative of Isaiah's. If so, I would imagine that the initial shock of the king's death was followed by grief. There must have been a period of intense mourning. I wonder if Isaiah experienced what King David felt when he poignantly revealed, "I am worn out from groaning; all night long I flood my bed with weeping and drench my couch with tears."[4]

Have you flooded your bed with weeping and drenched your couch with tears? Have you recently experienced the death of a loved one? Has unspeakable suffering penetrated your world? Or are you experiencing…

the living death of divorce?

the dreaded diagnosis of a debilitating, life-threatening disease?

the insurmountable distance that separates you from a friend?

the invisible barrier of hard feelings built by ...

disagreement

or jealousy

or misunderstanding

or deception

or the brokenness of betrayal ...

that walls you off in a world of isolated misery? Do you find yourself exhausted, just from emotional pain and grief? Do you sometimes feel that you just can't take *one more thing*? Even in your misery, be mindful that the very weight of your burdens and the intensity of the pressure may be exactly what God is going to use in your life to trigger an experience of personal revival. God may be preparing your heart for a life-changing glimpse of His glory, but before that can happen your burden may get heavier and your pressure greater as you struggle on through your life-shaking event.

I wonder if Isaiah's burden was heavier because of the knowledge that Uzziah, as he had grown older, had allowed pride to rule his life until he was no longer useful or pleasing to God. Sin in Uzziah's life had separated him from his family, his friends, and from God's presence in the temple.[5] Was Isaiah's grief intensified as he experienced the hopeless, hollow-eyed, chilling knowledge that his loved one had died while being separated from God?

Have you experienced the emotional torment of having to watch helplessly as sin has dominated and destroyed the life of your loved one? Has your grief been intensified because after you've prayed earnestly, passionately, and continuously, your loved one became more and more separated and isolated from those around him or her until the door has finally closed to any reconciliation or restoration of relationships? The finality of that severance can be extremely, emotionally life-shaking for you.

"In the year that King Uzziah died" (6:1), Isaiah's life was not only shaken emotionally and personally, but added to his suffering was the fact that he may well have been shaken financially at the same time.

Shaken Awake by a Financial Storm

As we're assuming, based on Isaiah's later writings, that he lived in the king's palace, could it be that when Isaiah had a financial or material need, he simply went to King Uzziah, and Uzziah supplied it?

Even when Jotham, Uzziah's son, ruled as the interim king while illness confined his father to a separate palace, Isaiah's needs were very probably met generously. It may well be that Isaiah had never had to think about where his next meal was coming from, never wrestled to find affordable housing, never questioned if he could work a new pair of shoes into his budget, never wondered how he could afford tuition for his child's education. In fact, he may never have had to budget at all. Maybe he never even thought about finances. But now the king was dead, and the possibility exists that Isaiah's cash flow was suddenly cut off, shaking him financially in addition to everything else he had to endure.

Have you experienced a financial or material setback through ...

a job termination?

a business downsizing?

a divorce?

an investment loss?

a stolen inheritance?

an insufficient retirement plan?

an astronomical medical bill?

And has the financial setback come in addition to . . .

a car accident or a harassment incident?

a doctor's diagnosis or a parent's prognosis?

a home burned down or a parole turned down?

a friend's betrayal or a child's failure?

a baby's retardation or a brother's addiction?

a racial slur or a pink slip?

an angry threat or a vicious twister?

a flooded house or an unfaithful spouse?

a violent rape or a silent burglary?

There have been times in my life when trouble has seemed to come in multiple layers. This has been true especially in the months since my husband's retirement from dentistry. For the first time in our almost-forty-years of marriage, we are trying to live within a set budget. Unexpectedly, our limited income has been strained in a recent six-week period when my husband had to have a heart catheterization with three stents inserted into his arteries. He also had three laser surgeries on his eyes for diabetic retinopathy, and he was diagnosed with sleep apnea and is now trying to adjust to sleeping with a mask strapped to his face. And while he has struggled to cope with one challenge after another, I have traveled to two cities for a major series of meetings, overseen strategic personnel adjustments on our ministry team, had the flu three times, and struggled through sleepless nights as I adjusted to a husband adjusting to his sleep machine. And in the midst of all these challenges, I began writing this book! Oh yes, and our son moved back home to live with us temporarily, and our granddaughter celebrated her third birthday!

There are days when I feel I can't keep my head above water. These life-shaking events seem to pile up stress and struggles, pressure and problems, every place I go and in every relationship I have — especially when added to the daily adjustment of living on a budget for the first time.

This time of personal and financial turbulence has served to create a high level of expectation in my heart. Since I know God loves me and is in control of all things, I also know this current round of multiple challenges I'm facing must mean that *He is up to something. What is it?*

Whatever it is, I know He's telling me I need to wake up! I need to adjust my attitude, stop feeling sorry for myself, stop complaining in my spirit, stop demanding that He bring relief, and begin to look at my situation from His perspective. I need to open the eyes of my heart and begin to search the "storm clouds" for the message within.

As horrific and evil and ugly and obscene as personal, emotional, financial, and any other type of suffering may be, I strongly suspect God wants to use it to get my attention! Whatever it is that is shaking your life and mine just may be the trumpet blast that heralds God's wake-up call to us, leading to personal revival! Because remember, it was during that difficult time, "in the year that King Uzziah died" (6:1), that Isaiah saw the Lord!

Don't Miss the Message

On December 17, 1903, Orville and Wilbur Wright sent a telegram from North Carolina's outer banks to their father, Bishop Milton Wright, in Dayton, Ohio, sharing what they knew was history-making news about their astonishing accomplishment. The message, written in the no-frills form of the telegraph, said, SUCCESS FOUR FLIGHTS THURSDAY MORNING ALL AGAINST TWENTY ONE MILE WIND STARTED FROM LEVEL WITH ENGINE POWER ALONE AVERAGE SPEED THROUGH AIR THIRTY ONE MILES LONGEST 57 SECONDS INFORM PRESS HOME CHRISTMAS.

Bishop Wright apparently sent the message to another adult son, Lorin, who shared it with Frank Tunison, a reporter for the Associated Press and the *Dayton Journal*. Tunison got the information — but he didn't "get" its importance. He didn't think the Wright brothers' feat was anything newsworthy, so he mentally "slept" through what would surely prove to be one of the biggest news events of his career.

But back in North Carolina, the lowly telegraph operator *did* understand the message. And even though the Wright brothers had asked him not to tell anyone (because they wanted the news to come from their hometown), he couldn't keep the amazing report to himself. As a result, the first reports of the Wright brothers' history-making flight appeared in newspapers in Cincinnati, New York, and Virginia and not in their own hometown publication.

The Dayton reporter had been given the scoop on perhaps the biggest single story of the twentieth century — man's first flight — but he had totally missed the message![6]

When disaster strikes, whether it's national, such as a destructive hurricane or the 9/11 attack on America; or personal, such as divorce, death, or disease; or economic, such as a job layoff or a stock market crash or a recession; or any other mortal, emotional, or financial storm, it's critical that you and I look up! Don't miss the message! *God may be calling...*

The apostle John testified that "Isaiah ... saw Jesus' glory and spoke about him."[7] When Isaiah's life was shaken by God's wake-up call, as incredible as it may seem from his Old Testament perspective, his eyes were opened to a fresh vision of God in the pre-incarnate[8] person of Jesus Christ. He didn't miss the message that was in the storm.

Several years ago, my father went through repeated surgeries for hydrocephalus. Shunts were inserted in his head to drain the fluid that was putting pressure on his brain, causing Parkinson's disease – type symptoms. His stay in the hospital was extended, and there were times when he genuinely believed his entrance into heaven was imminent. I have heard him recount on several occasions to family members and close friends that those days in the hospital that were filled with emotional and physical trauma were also filled with an acute awareness of God's presence. He has described those days as being intensely spiritual and worshipful as he believes God came down into that hospital room and gave him a fresh touch from heaven. As I observe the renewed physical strength of his body, the calm peace in his heart, and the radiant joy on his face, I believe him.

If your life is being shaken, get ready for what very well may be a life-changing experience of personal revival. This may be the very wake-up call God uses to open your eyes to the vision of His glory.

Whatever Isaiah was doing or whatever he was thinking or however he was affected, when he received the news of Uzziah's death, I don't think in his wildest dreams it ever occurred to him that this personal, emotional, financial, radical, life-shaking experience signaled a dramatic, impending, life-changing vision when his eyes were opened and he could say, "I saw the Lord."

But it did . . .

THREE

Open Your Eyes!

Isaiah 6:1–4

The Lord is much more than you know.

Carole's Story

On a cold, snowy night in Fargo, North Dakota, I saw the Lord! The vision came as I listened to Anne Graham Lotz present a message from God's Word describing Isaiah's experience of personal revival.

Anne's words gave me a totally fresh perspective. I realize now that my Bible studies and my daily devotions at that point in my life were largely focused on Jesus as Emmanuel—God with us, God with me. I was seeing Him largely as the Lord of my day-to-day life. As comforting as that reality is, I was missing so much more by not dwelling on His majesty. I was missing the awe that comes in recognizing Him as King, seated on the throne of not just my little life but of all creation.

The best example of what I am describing is my reaction to having met President George W. Bush just a year earlier when he came to a small gathering of technology executives. A colleague and I attended the meeting to represent our company and to present our software application as a way to help the nation's emerging energy crisis, which had been marked most recently by the California blackouts. After our presentation to him and the brief dialogue that followed, my colleague and I left feeling struck by how personable he was. He seemed genuinely interested in our solution, he asked insightful questions, and he was warm and very engaging. On the way out, I remarked to my colleague, "He is so easy to talk to, it was like meeting with one of my brothers." I went on to share how I almost had to intentionally remind myself during the exchange not to become overly "familiar" or casual in the conversation so I wouldn't forget I was talking to the leader of the free world.

The memory of that meeting helped me realize I had become so "familiar" with Jesus in my daily life that I had lost sight of the fact that He is the King of the universe.

In a manner that I now have come to realize is a signature of her writing and speaking, during her presentation Anne used words to paint a picture in my mind of the scene described early in Isaiah 6. Not using emotional language but a clear description of what Isaiah saw, it was as if Anne's words took me into God's temple. Suddenly I forgot I was sitting in a cavernous church sanctuary on a snowy night in North Dakota with hundreds of other people. Instead, I felt as though I were sitting right at the foot of the throne. Following Anne's words, I tracked every aspect of that scene in detail: the wings of the angels, the glorious smoke, the magnificently long robe that filled every inch of the temple, and the singing that shook the foundations.

By night's end, like never before, I saw the Lord seated on the throne—EXALTED.

~:~

Knowing God as He Truly Is

Years ago, at the conclusion of an address I had delivered to a large, national, secular audience, the master of ceremonies stood behind the podium and responded in a scathingly condescending voice, "Mrs. Lotz, we think you need to understand something. We all have our own god. Some of us call him Buddha, some of us call him Mohammed, some of us call him Messiah, and some of us may call him Jesus." As he sat down and the program ended, I left, thinking to myself, *But I don't want to know God like that.* I don't want to know God by the names other people call Him. I don't want to know Him according to what someone . . .

> says He might be like
>> or thinks He might be like
>>> or was taught He might be like
>>> or guesses He might be like
>>>> or even wishes He was like.

I want to know Him as He truly is. If there is a God in heaven, then surely He has a name He calls Himself. I want to know that name. And if there is a God in heaven, then He must have an intellect and emotions and will. I want to know His character and His personality. I want *to know Him*, not just know *about Him* in some secondhand, third-person way!

I'm not satisfied with a smorgasbord of opinions. I want to know the truth. About heaven. About hell. And most of all, about God. But . . .

> how can anyone know God?
> how can a finite person know the Infinite?
> how can a human being know the Divine?
> how can a mortal know the Immortal?
> how can this little dust person know the Eternal?
>> How can one who is confined by gravity to

planet earth know the One who holds the stars in His hands? It's ludicrous to even think such thoughts or have such a desire. Unless . . . God chooses to reveal Himself to humankind — to you . . . and to me.

And wonder of wonders, God *has* chosen to reveal Himself!

The apostle John declared that "God is light,"[1] and the primary characteristic of light is that it reveals itself. So John was announcing the thrilling news that God has revealed Himself to humankind in two primary ways: the written revelation we call the Bible, and the living revelation we know as Jesus Christ.

There is one, true, living God who created all things and who controls all things — a God who has chosen to reveal Himself to you and to me. We just need to wake up and open our eyes to Him.

Seeing God for Yourself

How do you and I open our eyes to the Invisible? We can't! Not on our own. God has to help us, but at the same time we have to be willing to allow Him to work in our lives. And the eyes that need to be opened are not the eyes in our head, but the eyes of our heart.

I wonder ... is God wanting to reveal His glory to you, but you're not "seeing"? Are you focused instead on pressures and problems, unable to see that they are just the wrappings on the outside of the "package" that contains a fresh encounter with Him?

I have a dear friend who is known for the spectacular way she wraps and presents her gifts. She uses yards and yards of ribbon for elaborate bows, and the gift wrap is always perfectly creased and matched. Her package decorations are gifts in themselves. Her theory is that it doesn't matter how tacky or ordinary the gift is inside the package — the recipient will be thrilled just by the appearance. And she is right! I'm always excited to receive one of her gorgeous packages, but at the same time, I remember that some of the most priceless gifts I've ever received have come in very ordinary wrappings.

For my birthday one year, my mother sent me a package wrapped in plain brown paper. When I opened it, there was a gaudy, multicolored

Mexican straw basket inside, stuffed with tissue paper. I actually thought my mother had totally lost her good senses! I tossed out the tissue paper, wondered what in the world I was going to do with the basket, then called to thank her for her "gift." Mother laughed when I thanked her for the basket then asked what I thought about what was inside it. I told her that nothing was inside except tissue paper, and I had thrown that out. She responded urgently, "Oh, no, Anne! Inside that tissue paper is your real birthday gift!"

I ran outside, opened up the trash can, and went through the garbage piece by piece until I came up with the wad of tissue paper. Inside was a small gold ring with a lapis lazuli stone that had been taken from the flooring in the Palace of Shushan and obtained from the British Museum![2] I had thrown out a priceless treasure simply because of the way it was wrapped!

What priceless treasure are you in danger of throwing out, simply because of the way it is packaged? Could it be the treasure of *seeing Him*? Sometimes God wraps His glory in hard circumstances or ugly obstacles or painful difficulties, and it just never occurs to us that within those life-shaking events is a fresh revelation of Him.

In the Old Testament, God wrapped His glory in an earthly tent that from the outside must have appeared, if not ugly, then certainly very ordinary. The tent was called the tabernacle,[3] and it housed the manifestation of His presence when the children of Israel wandered in the wilderness. God instructed them to cover the tabernacle itself with layers of goat hair and ram skins and even sea-cow hides![4] A casual observer would never have suspected that there would be any glory *there*! Yet the *Shekinah*[5] glory of God was revealed within this inauspicious and humble covering.[6]

Is God trying to pry open the eyes of your heart so He can show you His glory? Is He using a personal, emotional, or financial life-shaking experience you are enduring for that purpose? And have you misunderstood so that, the more intense your situation becomes, the more tightly you squeeze your eyes shut against Him and what He is trying to reveal to you? Are you so focused on the outer wrappings ...

the pressure and the problems,

the stress and the struggles,

the attack and the affliction,

the suffering and the sorrow,

the failure and the fatigue,

the mundane and the routine,

the responsibilities and the relationships,

the injustice and the unfairness,

the loss and the grief,

the "what ifs" and the "if onlys,"

that you are in danger of missing or even throwing away the fresh, personal revelation of Himself that He wants to give you?! And if you miss what He is trying to give you this time, what will He have to do to get your attention the next time?

Stop resisting Him. Stop resenting Him. Stop complaining. Stop feeling sorry for yourself. Stop demanding what you want. Stop focusing on the outer wrappings of yourself and your circumstances. Adjust your attitude. Change your mind about things — about yourself — about others — about Him. Relax in total trust. He knows what He's doing. Unwrap the package! Let go, and look up! Let Him open the eyes of your heart. OPEN YOUR EYES! *Open your eyes* to the vision of His glory! Prayerfully, expectantly, sincerely, open your eyes to Him!

Isaiah did. In the midst of his personal, emotional, financial, life-shaking experience, he opened his eyes and exclaimed, "In the year that King Uzziah died, *I saw the LORD*" (6:1).[7] His exclamation seems to reverberate through the ages, lifting his words right off the page as his spirit was launched to soar far out into the stratosphere of the eternal world, into the very throne room of heaven.

Praise God! If Isaiah could have such a vision, why can't I? So when the attack is furious, and the pressure is unrelenting, and the pain is unbearable, my spirit is on tiptoe as my heart whispers, *God, what are You going to reveal to me? What do You have for me inside this package? My eyes are wide open!*

Open the Eyes of Your Heart to His Power

When Isaiah opened his eyes and exclaimed, "I saw the LORD seated on a throne" (6:1), his vision was even more thrilling because it was a revelation of God ... *in the person of Jesus Christ*![8] And the fact that Isaiah saw Jesus seated on the throne was significant, because it revealed that Jesus Christ was in absolute authority of all that was taking place in the universe, on planet earth, in the nation of Judah, and in Isaiah's own personal life. Isaiah's eyes were opened to the power and the authority and the sovereignty of the Son of God.

There have been times when I have been tempted to doubt that Jesus sits on the throne, in control of *everything*. When my twenty-eight-year-old son called and calmly stated, "Mom, I have cancer," I cried, "Jesus, are You on the throne?"

When that same son, seven years later, called, and in a flat, strained voice said, "Mom, I've been to the attorney and filed for divorce," I cried again, "Jesus, are You still on the throne?"

In all honesty, at the conclusion of each of those phone calls, immediately the eyes of my heart were opened, and I "saw" Jesus seated on the throne, in absolute control of the events that seemed like huge tsunami waves crashing onto the shore of my life. I knew that while I was helpless in myself, I could lay hold of One who is mighty and whose faithfulness surrounds Him.[9] I knew with certainty that He was working out

His purpose, that it would be a far greater purpose than my mind could conceive,[10] that if I would just believe then I would see His glory,[11] and that I was to simply trust Him when I didn't understand why.[12] Knowing that He is on the throne, in control of everything, gives me peace and security. I know my life is not spinning randomly in some meaningless spiral; it has an eternal purpose He is working out for my good and His glory.[13]

What has caused you to doubt that Jesus sits on the throne? Do you question His absolute authority because some bad, unexpected thing has happened? Are you blinded to the vision of Him standing at the center of the universe in complete control of all that is taking place in your life? What is keeping your eyes tightly shut?

When the military police car pulled into your drive and two officers got out, knocked on your door, and said, "We are sorry to inform you...," did you cry out, "Jesus, are You on the throne?"

When your unmarried teenage daughter came home and told you she was pregnant, did you cry out, "Jesus, are You on the throne?"

When the sheriff's deputy called and said your son had been arrested for selling drugs, did you cry out, "Jesus, are You on the throne?"

When your husband retired and within the year was diagnosed with a terminal illness, did you cry out, "Jesus, are You on the throne?"

When your wife was left paralyzed by a drunk driver, did you cry out, "Jesus, are You on the throne?"

When you returned from work to find an eviction notice tacked to your apartment door, did you cry out, "Jesus, are You on the throne?"

Isaiah's testimony answers your gut-wrenched cry, "Yes! Yes! *YES! Jesus Christ, the Lord God, is on the throne! I saw Him seated there!*" And just in case you or I would say that that was then but not now, at the end of human history, remember that the apostle John underscored

Isaiah's vision when he too exclaimed, "I looked, and there before me was a door standing open in heaven.... And there before me was a throne in heaven with someone sitting on it."[14] *Jesus Christ is still seated on the throne!*

Have your tears blinded you to the vision of the power of Christ that He wants to give you at this very moment? Are you like Mary Magdalene early on that Sunday morning following the crucifixion of Jesus? As she peered into the empty recesses of the tomb, Mary was heartbroken and grief-stricken as she concluded that, not only had Jesus been crucified and buried, but His grave had been robbed and His body stolen. Then "she turned around and saw Jesus standing there, but she did not realize that it was Jesus."[15]

Jesus was alive and present in Mary's life, yet she didn't know it! She must have been blinded by her tears of grief and confusion and helplessness and hopeless despair! The most dramatic evidence of God's power that has ever been displayed in human history was standing by her, and she was blinded to Him!

Could it be that Jesus is waiting patiently in *your* life to give you evidence of His power that has not been diluted or depleted since that first Easter morning? Are you so focused on whatever your situation is, which looks so radically different from what you had imagined, that you can't see Him? Have your tears blinded you to Him? Are you so focused on your own pain or grief or confusion or helplessness or hopelessness that you are missing out on the greatest blessing you will ever receive? Could it be, at this very moment in your life, that Jesus is *right there with you*?

When Isaiah looked up, perhaps through eyes that were also swimming with tears, he saw the Lord, not only seated on a throne, but "high" (6:1).

Open the Eyes of Your Heart to His Position

The highest position in our nation is that of the presidency. Because the United States is the leader of the world, the office of president is arguably the highest position in the world. The one who is elected to that position holds it for four or possibly eight years and then fades onto the golf course, the after-dinner-speech club, or a book tour. But Jesus Christ, the Lord God of Isaiah's vision, holds the highest position, not just in the United States or on planet earth, but in the entire universe! And not just for four years or eight years but forever and ever and ever! He will never be voted out of office. He will never be ousted or overthrown! He will never retire or age out.

Because He holds the highest position in the universe forever and ever, I will never be condemned![16] My hope is sure![17] My future is secure![18] His promises are good![19]

If He says God loves me, *God loves me.*[20]

If He says I'm forgiven, *I'm forgiven.*[21]

If He says I'm God's child, *I'm God's child.*[22]

If He says I have eternal life, *I have eternal life.*[23]

If He says His Spirit lives in me, *His Spirit lives in me.*[24]

If He says I have the power to overcome, *I have the power to overcome.*[25]

If He says my life has eternal significance, *my life has eternal significance.*[26]

If He says I'm welcome in heaven, *I'm welcome in heaven.*[27]

Praise God! There is no higher final authority in all the universe than Jesus! What He says is so. When I call on Jesus, I am calling on the highest authority there is — anywhere!

At His Word ...

> the light shines,[28]
>
> the world spins,[29]
>
> the winds cease,[30]
>
> the demons flee,[31]
>
> the mountains fall,[32]
>
> the lame walk,[33]
>
> the deaf hear,[34]
>
> the blind see,[35]
>
> the lepers are cleansed,[36]
>
> the dead are raised,[37]
>
> and heaven is opened for you and me![38]

Praise God! *Praise God! PRAISE GOD!* When my life is shaken, my eyes are opened to the power of Christ and the position of Christ and the person of Christ!

Open the Eyes of Your Heart to His Person

In a voice still pulsating with the thrill of the revelation, Isaiah rejoiced, "I saw the LORD ..., exalted" (6:1). Not only does Jesus Christ hold the highest position in the universe, He is the greatest person in the universe! No person or thing is greater than He is.

God's people in Judah needed a fresh, clear vision of His greatness because they had become fascinated with other gods, falling so far away from the truth that they actually became involved in idolatry. They had adopted the foreign gods of the nations around them, substituting superstition and falsity for true worship of the living God.[39]

Their fascination with other gods was even more astounding because no nation on earth had experienced the one, true, living God to the extent that Judah had.[40] God had ...

> delivered His people from bondage in Egypt with a mighty hand,[41]
>
> opened up the Red Sea for them to cross on dry ground,[42]
>
> destroyed supernaturally Pharaoh's pursuing army,[43]
>
> fed them with manna in the wilderness,[44]
>
> quenched their thirst with water from a rock,[45]
>
> given them the unique revelation of Himself through the law, sacrifices, and ceremonies,[46]
>
> rolled back the Jordan River to give them dry passage into the Promised Land,[47]
>
> caused the walls of Jericho to crumble,[48]
>
> delivered the enemy into their hands through victory after victory,[49]
>
> and blessed them with a land flowing with milk and honey.[50]

He raised up prophets and priests and kings to lead them rightly.[51]

> He gave them His Word that they might know Him truly.[52]
>
> > He gave them His heart that they might love Him only.[53]
> >
> > > He gave them His Son that ultimately they might live with Him eternally.[54]

Despite all this, Judah, God's people called by God's name, rejected Him ... neglected Him ... snubbed Him ... defied Him ... disobeyed Him ... forsook Him as they flirted with other gods then gave themselves over to them. Without question, Judah needed a clearly defined, sharply focused vision of His greatness.

So do you and I — God's people who call ourselves by God's name living in the world today, as we toy with other gods — gods of ...

materialism and humanism,

sports and sex,

crystals and commerce,

pleasure and power,

drugs and alcohol,

science and technology,

Allah and Buddha and Mohammed and Krishna and Confucius ...
gods who are not gods at all but superstitions and lies that have become
attractive even to those within the church because we have lost our
vision of the greatness of our God!

In recent years, proponents of religious pluralism have gone so far
as to use my father's participation in a national worship service to
validate their compromise of the truth. The memorial service held at
the National Cathedral in Washington, DC, following the September
11 attacks featured Jewish, Muslim, and Christian religious leaders,
including my father. Those who promote their belief that all religions
are equally true have used my father's participation in this multifaith
service to challenge his commitment to the singular truth of the gospel.
My response is that my father was invited to participate in the program; he did not plan it. There is a vast difference. Not one of the thousands of meetings my father has planned and held around the world
ever featured someone of another religion praying, preaching, singing,
or reading Scripture.

Living in a changing world that at times uses ...

pluralism as a rationale for the worship of other gods,

and multiculturalism as an excuse to deny the truth,

and political correctness to silence the gospel,

those of us who call ourselves by God's name need a fresh vision of the
greatness of Jesus Christ. Maybe that's one very legitimate reason why

God has allowed our world to be shaken ... so that we would look up and see the Lord!

It's just that at times, even when we choose to open our eyes, He seems hard to see, doesn't He?

Open the Eyes of Your Heart to His Presence

Do you feel separated from God? Do you sometimes feel that He is way up there and you are way down here? Have you ever felt that there was a great gulf between you? Have you ever felt abandoned by Him? Then, like me, you need to learn to rest your faith, not in your feelings, but in the Word of God.

There have been times in my spiritual journey when my feelings have crowded out any awareness of God's presence in my life. I have felt abandoned by Him. At such times of weakness I have needed a clear vision of Jesus. I have needed to open my eyes to His presence in my life — a vision that He has given me through His Word, which distinctly promises, "Never will I leave you; never will I forsake you."[55]

As Isaiah continued to take in the vision that was unfolded before him, he observed that "the train of his robe filled the temple"(6:1). Obviously, there was no place where Jesus was not![56] The omnipresence of Jesus Christ is an enormous comfort to His children.

Think about it for a moment:
in the mountainous caves of Afghanistan,
in the bloodied streets of Israel,
in the drug-infested jungles of Colombia,
in the death camps of North Korea,
in the refugee camps of Palestine,
in the slave camps of the Sudan,
in the dehumanizing slums of Calcutta,
in the glittering palaces of Saudi Arabia,

in the children's orphanages of Romania,
in the AIDS hospitals of South Africa,
in the sleek boardrooms of America,
in the degrading bedrooms of Thailand ...
"The Lord is there."[57]

And the Lord is *here* — in this place — and in my heart. My eyes have been opened to the fact that I am, as a child of God, uniquely His temple.[58] Because when I came to God by faith, confessed and repented of my sin, asked Him to forgive and cleanse me with the blood of Jesus, and opened up my heart, inviting Him to come live within me, He accepted the invitation! He came in, in the person of the Holy Spirit. My body became His dwelling place — His temple.

I wonder — do you have that same assurance? Do you know that the Lord is there — in your heart? How do you know that for sure? He is a gentleman and will only come into your heart when you invite Him. When did you invite Him?

If you have not invited Him into your heart, then He's not there! There is no possibility of personal revival because there's no spiritual life to revive.

I don't want to assume, just because you are reading this book, that the Lord is there — in your heart. I have been teaching the Bible for thirty years, and I have encountered hundreds of men and women who have assumed they were Christians ...

because they were good,
or because they were members of a church,
or because they were raised in a Christian home,
or because they were not Muslim or Jewish,
or because they loved Jesus,
or because they just "felt" like a Christian,

but they had never deliberately made a conscious transaction of faith with God — a transaction when they confessed and repented of their sin, claimed Jesus as their personal Savior and Lord, received Him into their hearts, and were thus born again into God's family as God's children.

When have you made that deliberate transaction? If you are not sure that you ever have, would you do that right now? Open the eyes of your heart to see Jesus as more than just a man or a philosopher or a revolutionary or a great prophet.

See Him as God wrapped in human flesh, dressed in homespun and sandals ...

See Him giving His life as an atoning sacrifice for your sin on the Cross in order to offer you forgiveness and a right relationship with God ...

See Him as the risen Lord, shattering death and the grave in order to offer you eternal life ...

See Him here, now, gently whispering to your heart, *I love you. Please invite Me to live right there ... in your heart ... forever.*

If you have opened your eyes, if you have seen Him as your Savior and Lord and you long for His presence in your life, then pray this prayer sincerely, by faith:

Dear Jesus, I see who You are. For the first time, I really see You. You are the Creator who became my Savior. I earnestly want Your presence in my life. I know I am not worthy to be Your temple. I am a sinner, and I'm sorry. But I believe You died for me, and I am asking you to forgive me and cleanse me with Your blood. And I believe You rose up from the dead to give me eternal life. So right now, I'm asking You to give me eternal life. I open up my heart and invite You to come live within me. I surrender all that I am and all that I have and all that I know to Your authority. Amen.

If that is your sincere prayer of faith, then praise God! Open your eyes to the vision He now gives you of *you*! His Word says you now are forgiven of any and all sin,[59] you now have eternal life,[60] you now have Jesus living in your heart in the person of the Holy Spirit,[61] and you now are an authentic child of God![62]

Praise God! *Praise God!* Jesus is now present in your life, living in your heart, never to leave or forsake you! *PRAISE GOD!*

My eyes were opened to Him as my Savior when I was a little girl. I prayed a similar prayer, but with a child's words and a child's understanding. Yet I was sincere, and my faith was firmly planted in His Word. So I believe that, by His grace and mercy, I was truly born again into His family at that time.

Isaiah testified that he saw not only the presence of Jesus *in* the temple but the presence of Jesus *filling* the temple. In the same way, my eyes have been opened, not only to Jesus *in* my heart and life, but to Jesus *filling* my heart and life. In fact, He has commanded me to "be filled with the Spirit."[63]

What does that mean?

To be filled with His Spirit is to be moment-by-moment surrendered to His moment-by-moment control in my life. The result is that I am increasingly His look-alike and His act-alike and His live-alike. It means that the beautiful facets of His glorious nature — His love and His joy and His peace and His patience and His kindness and His goodness and His faithfulness and His gentleness and His self-control — are more and more obvious in my life, obvious even to those who know me best and live closest to me and work side by side with me.

It means that this private woman, this shy housewife and mother, has been given a holy boldness to stand up for Jesus when the occasion demands it. It means that this poor, stammering tongue is loosed to speak out for Jesus, presenting His truth and love in such a way that lives are changed.[64]

And if He can transform me through the fullness of His Spirit, He can transform you! My eyes have been opened, not only to a vision of the Spirit of Jesus filling this temple, but also of filling the church as He fills each and every individual within it. If Jesus could turn the world upside down with twelve disciples who were filled with the Holy Spirit, can you imagine what He could do today if every person who claims to be born again into God's family were filled with the Spirit?![65] And so I pour out my life in arenas and convention centers, before thousands and before one, in public and in private, seeking to bring God's people, who are called by God's name, into a fresh encounter with Him, so that their eyes are opened.

Can you imagine the difference it would make in your neighborhood if every church were filled with people who were filled with the Spirit of Jesus? Can you imagine the difference it would make in your town if every church in every neighborhood were filled with people who were filled with the Spirit of Jesus? Can you imagine the difference it would make in your region if every church in every neighborhood in every town in your region were filled with people who were filled with the Spirit of Jesus? Can you imagine the difference it would make in your nation if every church in every neighborhood in every town in every region were filled with people who were filled with the Spirit of Jesus? *Can you imagine the difference it would make in our world if every church in every neighborhood in every town in every region in every nation were filled with people who were filled with the Spirit of Jesus?*

That's the vision Isaiah was given of the presence of the Lord, a vision he expressed by exclaiming, "The train of his robe filled the temple."

And that's the vision needed today, beginning right here. Right now. With me. With you. We need to surrender our lives totally, without reservation, to the authoritative, loving, wise, moment-by-moment control of His Spirit.

What is keeping you from making such a decision? Don't let pride or doubt or unbelief or fear or the opinions of others or weary complacency keep you from unleashing the fullness of God's blessing. Yield yourself totally to Him.

Open the Eyes of Your Heart to His Praise

While Isaiah must have been contemplating the thrill of worldwide revival and the eternal repercussions of the temple being filled with God's Spirit, he saw angels hovering above the throne, "each with six wings.... And they were calling to one another: 'Holy, holy, holy is the Lord Almighty; the whole earth is full of his glory'" (6:2 – 3).

Years later, another prophet, the apostle John, reveled in his own eyewitness account of the future. His eyes were opened to the end of human history as we have known it, a time when the entire universe will roar in acclamation of the One who alone is worthy: "The Lamb, who was slain, to receive power and wealth and wisdom and strength and honor and glory and praise!"[66] John testified that he "heard every creature in heaven and on earth and under the earth and on the sea, and all that is in them, singing: 'To him who sits on the throne and to the Lamb be praise and honor and glory and power, for ever and ever.'"[67] And the entire universe rocked in praise of Jesus!

As John surely listened in awe, I wonder, down on planet earth where the majority of the people were blaspheming the name of Christ and engaged in all manner of ungodliness and wickedness, did the world suddenly become eerily still and silent? Did the little dust creatures who had been shaking their little dust fists at God in some way hear what was taking place in the rest of the universe? And because "God exalted him to the highest place and gave him the name that is above every name," was it at this moment that "every knee should bow, in heaven and on earth and under the earth, and every tongue confess that Jesus Christ is Lord, to the glory of God the Father"?[68]

Who do you know who has set himself or herself against Christ ... a coworker? ... a family member? ... a school board? ... a professor? ... an employer? ... a political party? ... a governmental system? ... *an entire culture?*

One day the entire world will set itself against Christ! But sooner or later, those who set themselves against Him will end up on their faces before Him. Because God gives you and me the right to choose Jesus as Savior — or reject Him. But He gives us no right to choose whether or not we will acknowledge Him as Lord. One day, *everyone* will acknowledge Him, whether they want to or not, and the entire universe will resound with unbounded praise of the One who alone is worthy: the Lord, seated on a throne, high and exalted, with the train of his robe filling the temple! Jesus is Lord of all!

As Isaiah heard the unbounded praise of Jesus Christ echoing throughout the universe, he noted that "at the sound of their voices the doorposts and thresholds shook and the temple was filled with smoke" (6:4). When ... unrestricted ... unhindered ... unbridled ... unabridged ... unlimited praise of Jesus Christ resounds throughout the hearts and lives and lips of His people, things begin to happen! As at Pentecost, when the Holy Spirit came down in fullness upon God's people, they opened their mouths to praise Jesus and proclaim the gospel, and three thousand people were converted in one day![69]

Oh, for another Pentecost!

Has anything interrupted your praise of Christ?

Your feelings?

Your fears?

Your failures?

Your doubts?

Your desires?

Your debts?

Your pain?

Your problems?

Your pleasures?

Your marriage?

Your memories?

Your misery?

Your tears?

Your temptations?

Your tiredness?

Your busyness?

Your barrenness?

Your brokenness?

Your loneliness?

Your singleness?

Your helplessness?

Your weakness?

Your weariness?

Your worries?

Whatever is interrupting your praise, would you take it to Jesus in prayer? Perhaps you can ask someone else to pray with you and for you — then make a list of every characteristic of Jesus you can think of, and praise Him for who He is. Fill in the blank: *I praise You for Your*

_____.

The wonderful truth is that God draws near to us as we praise Him because He inhabits the praises of His people.[70] Praise is also a powerful antidote to depression.[71] It's one of the ways we overcome our enemies, within and without.[72] Praise changes our perspective.[73] *Praise Him!* How will you ever know the blessings that can flow into your life as you praise Him, if you don't praise Him? *Start now!*

Isaiah saw that as the "temple" was saturated in praise, it was filled with "smoke." The smoke was not wood smoke but the *Shekinah* glory of God that came down. Isaiah would have been familiar with this "smoke." Although I doubt he had ever seen it personally before, he knew of it from the testimony of others. The history of Judah carefully recorded the glory of God that guided the Israelites through the wilderness for forty years. During the day God's glory took the form of a cloudy pillar that shielded His children from the scorching desert sun; at night His glory appeared as a fiery pillar to give them light in the darkness. Whenever and wherever the pillar moved, the Israelites followed because it represented the presence of God in their midst, leading them to the Promised Land.[74]

The smoke was clearly in evidence again when Moses went up on Mount Sinai to receive God's law. When he returned, having been in God's presence for over forty days and forty nights, the Israelites marveled and were afraid to come near him because his physical face reflected the radiant glory of God.[75] The same golden glory cloud filled the Tent of Meeting and the tabernacle so that not even Moses could enter.[76]

In a later generation following Moses' day, Ezekiel prophesied in a refugee camp as a slave in Babylon. He described the dramatic scene of God's glory being removed from the temple in Jerusalem because His people had sinned and were separated from Him, their praise having dried up like ashes in their mouths.[77]

The thrilling promise communicated by Isaiah's vision is that when you and I, as God's people, saturate our lives with genuine, uninterrupted, heartfelt praise, then the same glory that led the children of Israel through the wilderness, the same glory that was reflected on Moses' face, the same glory Ezekiel saw taken up from the temple, *comes down!*

And as astounding as it may seem, praise of Jesus Christ that is offered twenty-four hours a day, seven days a week, precedes the ultimate outpouring of God's glory on earth. When one day the sky unfolds and Jesus Christ returns to reign and rule in righteousness and justice, bringing peace on earth, He will come back to the thundering chorus of the voices "of many angels, numbering thousands upon thousands, and ten thousand times ten thousand.... In a loud voice [singing]" songs of praise to Jesus Christ![78]

I wonder ... what would be the impact on the world if the church — God's people, who are called by God's name — began to practice uninterrupted praise of Christ? Praise offered not just by the songs we sing or the words we speak but by the life we live — a life lived in the midst of a changing world that is increasingly hostile to the name of Jesus? Surely that kind of praise would be contagious and would compel others to want to know our Jesus, who provokes such unabashed adoration. *Oh, God, open my eyes to the powerful blessing of uninterrupted praise ... in my own life and flowing from my own lips!*

Open the Eyes of Your Heart to His Purity

The song that millions of angels will sing in heaven at the end of human history on earth is the same song Isaiah heard when he saw the Lord.[79] It was a song about the purity of Jesus Christ: "Holy, holy, holy is the LORD Almighty" (6:3).

Jesus Christ is absolutely pure . . .

in His methods and His motives and His manner.

He is absolutely pure . . .

in His deeds and His decisions and His directives.

He is absolutely pure . . .

in His actions and His attitude and His aim.

He is absolutely pure . . .

in His words and His will and His ways.

He is absolutely pure . . .

in His thoughts and His emotions and His judgments.

He has no hidden agenda . . . no ulterior motives . . . no selfishness or sinfulness *at all.* He is holy . . . holy . . . holy . . . *holy.*

And He demands holiness of His people![80] While you and I compare ourselves with each other and thus lower our standards, concluding, *I'm better than she is,* or *I'm not as bad as he is,* we forget that God's standards have not changed.

As evidence of the pure, unchanging standards of God's holiness, Jesus singled out a particular church, the church of Thyatira, for a stinging rebuke. Modern scholars wonder why a church so small in a town so obscure would receive our Lord's undivided attention in the last book of the Bible.[81] I believe his warning to Thyatira is also a solemn warning to those today who may think their lives are so small, so obscure, so insignificant, that they can get by with sin. They may be like the church at Thyatira; it had become so much like the surrounding world that the casual observer would have been hard pressed to tell the difference.

What was missing in the church that would provoke the wrath of the Son of God? *Holiness!*

Today there seems to be as much sin within the modern church as there was in that little church in Thyatira.

When performance is substituted for character,
　when activity is substituted for life,
　　when programs are substituted for prayer,
　when orthodoxy is substituted for obedience,
when traditions are substituted for the truth,
　when baptisms are substituted for conversions,
　　when religion is substituted for a personal relationship,
　when politics are substituted for power,
　　when personal agendas are substituted for His glory alone ...
it's only a matter of time before sin creeps into the church body.

You and I need to be careful! There are whole denominations that sanction sin! The sin may not be intentional; it may be that sin has just crept in generally unnoticed until it has become tolerated, accepted, and sometimes even promoted. But God's children need to be mindful that being influenced by what others say or do around us, even within the church, is not an acceptable excuse for sin. God will call you and me into account for the sin in our own lives, not someone else's. God is not mocked. He demands holiness and purity from His people!

Are you unconsciously substituting something for holiness? Is it positive thinking? Or modern-day morality? There is no substitute, from God's perspective. Like dust in a darkened room, sin often goes unnoticed until we turn on the Light, bringing God's Word into our lives.

Years ago, my father and mother were asked by a major talk-show host if they would grant a televised interview from their home. My parents agreed. Two weeks before the interview was to take place, Mother did what any self-respecting housewife would do: she began to clean the house furiously. With the help of several friends, Mother polished, waxed, washed, and dusted until the old log cabin we call home looked the best it ever had.

When the day came for the interview, Mother confidently greeted the talk-show host and his technical crew at the front door then led them into the living room. Within a short period of time, the room was transformed into a television studio with miles of cables crisscrossing the floor, huge television lights perched on tripods, and cameras placed strategically so views could be taken from every angle. As the host positioned my parents on the sofa, Mother was serenely poised. Looking about the room, she could see it was absolutely spotless. Even the cables, cameras, and equipment didn't mar the polished, waxed, washed, and dusted beauty.

Then the director said, "Lights, camera, action!" and the cameras began to roll as the huge television lights were turned on. In absolute horror, Mother looked around at her "spotless" room! She saw cobwebs in the corners of the old logs, soot in the fireplace, dust bunnies under the table — even dust in the air! Under ordinary lighting the room had looked perfectly clean, but under the intense television lights the dirt was revealed.

Mother's living room is like our lives. Under ordinary lighting, as we set our own standards, compare ourselves with others, do what feels good and what we think is right in our own eyes, we can be deluded into thinking we're okay. In fact, we can even think we are better than others, confident that God must be pleased with us.

Then we go to church or Sunday school, or get into a Bible study, or perhaps hear a Bible-based message, and the light of God's Word shines into our lives. Under the intensity of His light, we see things we had not seen before — the cobwebs of selfishness, the soot of secret sin, the dust of disobedience. Although the revelation can be horrifying, it can also be beneficial as it illuminates the "dirt" that must be confronted, confessed, cleansed, and corrected if we are to be holy as He is holy.

Has our study of God's Word turned on the Light in your life? Has the vision of the glorious power, position, person, presence, praise, and purity of Jesus made you feel bad? Dirty? Guilty? *Sinful?* Then be *encouraged*! The eyes of your heart are opening more fully.

Perhaps in a similar way, the "Light" shone in on Isaiah's life as his eyes were opened and he saw Jesus as He really is. And then, in the blinding purity and searing holiness of Christ, his eyes were opened to himself . . .

~ FOUR ~

Rend Your Heart!

Isaiah 6:5

He is so big . . . and we are so nothing.

Carole's Story

Sometimes we're faced with the multitude of sins in our life. But on this particular evening as I listened to Anne, the Lord showed me one predominant sin that had become a barrier to my spiritual pathway. In retrospect, I can see it was the primary obstacle that had been keeping me from seeing Him, as well as keeping me from seeing how much more He had for my life and how much more He expected from my service. When I arrived home that evening after hearing the message, that lone sin stared me in the face. I didn't even remember writing it in my Bible's margin during the service, but there it was, written in all caps: PRIDE.

In the sleepless hours that followed, I realized that while I did have Jesus in my life, I had far more of ME in it than Him. With that revelation, I saw my career and life success as more than simply the Lord's blessing. That night, in the light of God's glory, I saw my striving so hard to climb the corporate ladder for what it was: not something I did to bring God glory but a passion I pursued to gain worldly reward.

Seeing my motives for what they were that evening was disgusting. What had been gratifying and fulfilling just days earlier — the promotions, the position, the recognition — suddenly seemed of little value ...

A Nudge, Then a Whisper: "Look — He's Here"

Years ago I was in London with my father. We were just leaving the hotel together, accompanied by one of his aides, when we passed a very handsome, familiar-looking man coming through the door. I immediately recognized him as Hugh O'Brien, an actor who had starred in the *Wyatt Earp* television series for many years. My father stuck out his hand as he greeted him with, "Hugh, it's good to see you again."

Mr. O'Brien recognized Daddy also and stood briefly to chat. Daddy introduced him to me, then to his aide. His aide had heard only the name "Hugh," and with his face wreathed in smiles, he responded, "It's nice to meet you, Mr. Hefner!"

It was all I could do to keep a straight face until Mr. O'Brien had disappeared into the darkened recesses of the hotel lobby. Then, as Daddy and I burst out laughing, we explained, much to the chagrin of his aide, that he had just met Hugh O'Brien, not Hugh Hefner, founder of the *Playboy* empire! The only way Daddy's aide knew he had just met Hugh O'Brien was because we told him he had. Although he had seen Hugh O'Brien, he didn't recognize him for who he really was.

In traveling, there have been many times when I've been unaware that a notable person was nearby. Paul McCartney, Dick Morris, Richard Thomas, Prince, David Gergen, Richard Dean Anderson (who starred in the television series *MacGyver*), Cokie Roberts, Charlie Gibson, and many more would have all passed by me unnoticed except for my traveling companion, who has nudged me and whispered, "Anne, don't look now, but so-and-so is here. Right over there." And when I have looked "right over there," I have seen a very ordinary person. No glitz or glamour, no neon lights or fancy get-up, just another traveler struggling with his or her bags or trying to get comfortable in a seat that's too small while being gracious under the bold, scrutinizing stares of curious onlookers. Somehow seeing a famous celebrity in an ordinary setting is just, well, not that exciting.

I wonder ... would it be possible to see Jesus and not know it? As wildly implausible as it might seem, yes, it *is* possible. Like Mary Magdalene at the garden tomb on Easter morning, you and I may see Him yet not recognize Him.[1] Sometimes we need help. Someone to nudge us and whisper, "Look. He's here. Right over there."

Then, when we see Him for who He is, it's not what we expected ...

Rended by Helplessness

One reason I have been unaware at times that I was seeing Jesus was because the experience wasn't what I had thought it would be. I thought that seeing Jesus would send me into a kind of spiritual orbit. I thought it would result in a glorious, exhilarating, out-of-body ecstatic experience. Yet within seconds the thrill of a fresh encounter can morph from the heights of joy to the depths of depression. And the depression then seems to call into question the validity of the encounter. How could meeting Jesus make me feel so miserable and helpless?

It has been Isaiah's testimony that has nudged me, as though to say, *Anne, look. He's here. Right over there.* Isaiah has made me aware that I have seen Jesus many more times than I have realized. And the hallmark of having had an encounter with Jesus is not necessarily ecstasy.

In the year *before* Isaiah saw the Lord, he had passionately preached a message to the people in his changing world, exhorting them to repent of the six following sins, in particular:

"Woe to you who add house to house and join field to field till no
    space is left and you live alone in the land" (Isaiah 5:8).

"Woe to those who rise early in the morning to run after their
     drinks, who stay up late at night till they are inflamed with
     wine" (5:11).
"Woe to those who draw sin along with cords of deceit, and
     wickedness as with cart ropes" (5:18).
"Woe to those who call evil good and good evil" (5:20).
"Woe to those who are wise in their own eyes and clever in their
     own sight" (5:21).
"Woe to those who are heroes at drinking wine and champions
     at mixing drinks, who acquit the guilty for a bribe, but deny
     justice to the innocent" (5:22 – 23).

Woe to you. *Woe to you. WOE TO YOU!* Isaiah was preaching his
heart out, pointing his finger at the sin he saw in the society of his collapsing culture. And he was preaching God's truth!

Isaiah's no-holds-barred indictment of Judah in his day seems to
echo through the centuries, reverberating with relevancy right down
to our generation ...

*"Woe to you who add house to house and join field to field till no
space is left and you live alone in the land."* Woe to you who rob other
people's pensions to pad your own ... who build up your own business
by destroying that of others ... who greedily increase your profits at
any cost. *Woe to you.*

*"Woe to those who rise up early in the morning to run after their
drinks, who stay up late at night till they are inflamed with wine."* Woe
to those who are alcoholics, drug addicts, and chemically dependent.
Woe to you.

*"Woe to those who draw sin along with cords of deceit, and wickedness
as with cart ropes."* Woe to the religious hypocrite who is a Bible quoter

and a Bible toter, pretending to be more spiritual than he is while harboring secret sin in his heart or private life. *Woe to you.*

"Woe to those who call evil good and good evil." Woe to those who exchange the truth of God for a lie ... who switch the labels to make sin appear to be less offensive ... who call

lying — exaggeration,

unbelief — worry,

murder — a right to choose,

abomination — gay,

fornication — safe sex.

Woe to you.

"Woe to those who are wise in their own eyes and clever in their own sight." Woe to the proud and the arrogant and the self-promoting. *Woe to you.*

"Woe to those who are heroes at drinking wine and champions at mixing drinks, who acquit the guilty for a bribe, but deny justice to the innocent." Woe to those who live for pleasure and parties ... who have no integrity ... whose lives falsely convey character doesn't count. *Woe to you.*

Often when I watch the evening news or read the morning newspaper, I also have an overwhelming desire to point my finger and thunder, "Woe to you, woe to you, woe to you!"

My focus is entirely on *their* sin!

Before he saw the Lord, Isaiah had been totally focused on *their* sin too. But when he saw the Lord, his eyes were opened, not only to a fresh vision of who Jesus is, but to a fresh vision of himself. Then Isaiah wailed, "Woe to *me*!" (6:5). He wasn't ecstatic. He wasn't transported to heights of glory. He wasn't uplifted to an exalted spiritual plateau. In the words of the Old Testament prophet Joel, Isaiah was being challenged to "rend [his] heart and not [his] garments"[2] as he was plunged into a state of spiritual helplessness and depression.

Rended by Hopelessness

When Isaiah saw the Lord, he felt dirty. Sinful. Wretched. Guilty. Worthless. Ashamed. Isaiah's encounter was very much like the apostle Peter's experience...

When Peter saw Jesus, Peter didn't know who He really was, although he had actually met Jesus once before when his brother Andrew had introduced them. But one day Jesus climbed into Peter's fishing boat, preached to the crowd on the shore, then told Peter to take Him fishing. Peter resisted because he had been fishing all night and had caught nothing. "But because you say so, I will let down the nets," he said.[3]

When Peter obeyed Jesus, he took so many fish into his nets that they began to break. He quickly called for reinforcements, and the boat that came alongside to help haul in the catch quickly filled up until all its nets were breaking too. Then both boats began to sink.

Suddenly Peter knew he was in the presence of Someone who was more than just a man. The Light came on in Peter's life as his eyes were opened. But instead of making him feel good, it made him feel dirty as his sin was revealed. His knees buckled, and he fell at the feet of Jesus, crying, "Go away from me, Lord; I am a sinful man!"[4]

Isaiah, flooded by the light of holiness and purity that emanates from the Lord, had nowhere to hide and no one to blame. Isaiah knew then that he was not a victim; he was a sinner.

Think back in your life. When have you felt the acute weight and unshakable burden of your sin? When have you felt so spiritually poor and blind and naked and utterly helpless that you even despaired of life? Could it be, dear one, that *that* was your encounter with the spotless, sinless Son of God? *Could it be that the nearer to Him you actually are, the closer to hell you actually feel*[5] because your sin becomes glaringly apparent in the searing light of His holiness? Could it be that God is calling you to "rend your heart and not your garments"?[6]

When has that truth pierced your heart? At the point of that agonizing realization, did you squeeze the eyes of your heart tightly shut, deafen your ears, and run away in your spirit? Who was the "friend" God used to nudge you into His presence, into the light of His holiness, as though to say, "Look! He's here! Right over there." Was it your pastor as he delivered the Sunday morning sermon? And then did you run out of the sanctuary as quickly as you dared? Or was it a teacher sharing a message you heard in your weekly Bible study? And then did you drop out of the class? Was it your sister, who warned you with tears? And then did you abruptly depart from her house? Who has been your "friend," and how have you responded to his or her nudge?

Did you slam down the phone?

Take off the headset?

Throw down the remote?

Shut off the radio?

Cut off the relationship?

Anything to get away from the surgical knife
of conviction?

Have you been cowering behind arguments of self-defense and rationalization, covering up your quivering spirit with excuses for your sin while blaming someone else for it? Who have you been blaming for the sin in your life? . . . Your parents? . . . Your spouse? . . . Your environment? . . . Your lack of education? . . . Your financial straits? . . . Your business partner? . . . Your physical pain? . . . Your landlord?

Other people and circumstances may provoke you to sin and encourage you to sin and motivate you to sin, *but the choice to sin is your own.* When have you accepted responsibility for the sin in your own life? Stop blaming someone else, and cry out now, as Isaiah did, "Woe to me. I'm a sinner."

Isaiah not only accepted responsibility for his sin, he acknowledged that he was ruined by it. To his credit, he didn't shut his eyes or deafen his ears or whine about what somebody else did or didn't do; he didn't run away from the blinding light. Isaiah, in soul-stripping, brutal honesty, sobbed, "I am ruined!" (6:5). This was no shallow, superficial, hypocritical show of spirituality. This was the cry of a man whose heart had been rended in two.

Such a concept of utter spiritual ruination is almost foreign to our modern-day mind. So much of our focus seems to be on building up our self-esteem and thinking positively. We are repulsed by even the thought of being so totally helpless in our sinful condition that we are actually ruined by it and therefore spiritually hopeless, with not even a remote possibility of ever pleasing God. Never being right with Him. Forever unacceptable in His presence. Unwelcome in His heavenly home.

I was reminded recently of my ruined sinful state in a very painful way. Every year as December draws near I ask Jesus what He would like for His birthday. It usually takes days and even weeks for the answer to come in the form of an opportunity to pursue or an idea to implement or a service to render. One year I felt He asked me to write my first book, *The Vision of His Glory.* Another year it was to tell the Christmas story to my child's public-school class. Whatever it is each year, it is always something that is sacrificial in nature, something I wouldn't do except that He has impressed on my heart that it is the gift He wants.

This past year, I had prayed around the first of November, asking Him what He would like as a gift from me for His birthday. He had not yet answered me by early December when I was invited to a lovely Christmas luncheon in the home of a dear friend. As I drove to her home, my cell phone rang. It was my publicist calling to say a national television talk show had invited me to participate in a panel discussion. Live. That night. When I asked who else would be on the panel, she responded that she didn't know but would find out and get back to me.

I went on to the luncheon, and when it was over and I left, I had a voice-mail message on my cell phone from the publicist. I returned her call, and she informed me that I didn't have to be concerned; she had declined the opportunity for me because the panel was a very tough one. I felt a sense of relief, drove home, and immediately immersed myself in other responsibilities.

That night, as the time drew near for the program I had declined to appear on, I had the very sinking, sickening feeling that being on that show had been the Christmas gift Jesus had wanted me to give Him. As I actually watched the panel discussion and observed the woman they had put in "my place," I felt confirmed in it.

No amount of confession, apology, or tears could erase or even ease the knife of conviction and even self-loathing I experienced throughout the Christmas holidays. I knew, as I had raced in and out of that Christmas luncheon, that I had never stopped and prayed . . . I had never asked Jesus if the television opportunity was a door for service that He had opened . . . I had never asked Him if participating on that challenging panel was the gift He might have wanted for His birthday. And I knew in a very fresh way the reality of my ruined, sinful nature that is always so close to the surface in my life; it is a nature that has to be deliberately and consistently and constantly crucified and brought under submission to His authority, a sinful nature that is only conquered as I live surrendered moment-by-moment to the moment-by-moment control of the Holy Spirit. That nature is still such a powerful force in my life that in one unguarded moment, it had gotten the best of me.

As I reflect back on what I felt was a personal Christmas debacle — rushing around decorating and shopping and wrapping and celebrating, all under the pretense of keeping my focus on the real meaning of the holidays while I had turned a deaf ear to what He really wanted from me — it occurred to me that what He really wanted from me for His birthday was my *humility*. And so, on my knees with a heart that was rended and contrite, I cried out from *fresh experience,* "Woe to me!... I am ruined!" And I gave it to Him.

Rended by Humiliation

The apostle Paul had a similar overwhelming experience when he exclaimed, "I know that nothing good lives in me."[7] *Nothing good?!* In a man who penned almost half of the New Testament? In the Light of the holiness of Christ, Paul's self-esteem — and Isaiah's — and ours — crumbles into dust. When a person truly "sees" the Lord, there is no ...

> arm-waving,
>> hand-clapping,
>>> rhythm-swaying,
>>>> feet-dancing

response. Instead, there is an overwhelming sense of awe that is permeated with reverential fear. *And we fall down!*

In our own minds ... and hearts ... and wills ... in our own intellect ... and emotions ... and decisions, we "fall down" in humility at His feet.[8]

Isaiah gives testimony to the fact that, not only was he ruined himself in that he was a helpless sinner before a holy God, but he was ruined in his service. With stunning clarity he saw himself as never before, "a man of unclean lips." Isaiah was a prophet. His lips, as he preached God's Word, were the instruments of his service. I wonder if he had secretly believed the sin in his life was not as great as it was in the lives of others? Had he been pointing his finger in condemnation at the obvious sin in the lives of others while missing the more subtle sins in his own life?

I have recently witnessed an amazing spectacle within a church. The ruling board of elders condemned and sought to remove the church's young pastor for not returning phone calls and for not smiling when greeting worshipers and for breaking a luncheon appointment. While pointing the finger at the pastor, they totally ignored their own gossip, their critical spirits, their murmuring, and their complaining. They shredded the unity within the congregation, severed relationships of a lifetime, and diverted the energy of the church from its mission of preaching the gospel and making disciples. They filled the backrooms and the boardroom of the church with in-fighting, political maneuvering and power control — rending their garments as their lips dripped pious platitudes, all while saying the young pastor didn't have a loving, shepherd's heart! But where were the rended, broken, contrite hearts that are the hallmark of leaders who truly walk with God?[9]

Jesus searchingly inquired of those listening to His Sermon on the Mount, "Why do you look at the speck of sawdust in your brother's eye and pay no attention to the plank in your own eye? . . . You hypocrite, first take the plank out of your own eye, and then you will see clearly to remove the speck from your brother's eye."[10]

How is it that, like Isaiah, we can be so sensitive and offended and preoccupied with the sin of others as we rend our garments while we are blindly oblivious to the sin in our own lives and our hearts are unscathed? I wonder if this is one reason the world seems to view the church as a haven for hypocrites, because while the unsaved may be somewhat aware of the sin in their own lives for which we condemn them, they also see the sin in ours, which we ignore.

Ashamed

With a face that must have burned crimson with shame, Isaiah burst into a startled confession as he realized, "I am a man of unclean lips, and I live among a people of unclean lips, and my eyes have seen the King, the LORD Almighty" (6:5). In other words, "I'm no better than the people at whom I've been pointing my finger. I'm a sinner too. In the light of who He is — in the light of His holiness and righteousness and purity — I am helpless. I am hopeless. I am ruined myself and ruined in my service. *How can I ever be used of God when I'm no better than the people to whom I am preaching?*"

That was not just a humbling confession: it was a humiliating confession!

Isaiah's sins were not readily obvious — at least not to me as I thoughtfully read the first five chapters of his book. If his standards had been set . . .

> by the lifestyles and language of others,
>> by the attitude and actions of others,
>>> by the priorities and pleasures of others,

then in comparison he might have felt very confident in himself and in his service. But when his life was measured by the standards of perfect holiness, the revelation of sin was devastating!

Again and again as I stand to publicly proclaim God's Word, in my spirit I am on my face before God with a dreadful fear, acutely aware that I am a sinner, no better than those who look back at me with attentive, upturned faces. But when I began ministry, I lacked a Spirit-sensitized awareness of my own sinfulness.

Guilty

I remember being so spiritually superficial that when a speaker challenged those in the audience, including myself, to spend a few moments in confession of sin, I could not think of even one sin in my life to confess! But then I came across James 2:10, which issues this indictment, "For whoever keeps the whole law and yet stumbles at just one point is guilty of breaking all of it."

All of it? *All of it!* I thought of all the moments of all the days of all the weeks of all the months of all the years in my life when I had broken the greatest commandment — the one that directs me to love the Lord my God with all my heart, soul, mind and strength.[11] Since I was easily guilty of this sin, I was guilty of all sin. Why? Because just one sin reveals that I have what could be termed the "disease" of sin.

The reality of this disease of sin was illustrated to me one night when my third child, Rachel-Ruth, was small. She came running to me, struggling with her shirt and complaining that something had bitten her underneath it. I lifted up her shirt, and sure enough, there was a little red "bite." So I looked all through the shirt, found nothing, and told her whatever it was had gone, so she could go back and play. A few minutes later, she came running to me, exclaiming dramatically that she had been bitten again. When I lifted her shirt, this time I saw two red "bites." So I removed her shirt, checked her carefully for mosquitoes, spiders, or even fleas then put a clean shirt on her, assuring her she was fine. A few minutes later she again came running back to me, flinging herself into my arms, tearfully telling me that whatever it was had bitten her all over. When I examined her, I saw that she was covered in red "bites." Except they were not bites at all — Rachel-Ruth had the chicken pox!

Just as the first small spot indicated my daughter had the disease of chicken pox even though she had not broken out all over, one sin in your life or mine indicates we are riddled with the disease, even though we haven't broken out to the point that it's obvious to others — or even to ourselves. And in my life, just one moment of not loving God with all my heart is enough to clinch the verdict that I am a sinner.[12]

I hate sin, and I don't want to sin, but it's my nature to do it. And although I have victory over sin when I live in my new nature by the power of His Spirit, the sin I still commit makes me sick of myself.[13] Sometimes the sin is not obvious, and for that reason, from time to time, I need a wake-up call to personal revival — a fresh experience and vision of Christ in order to open my eyes to His holiness and my help-lessness and the eternal hope of the Cross. I need to come back to the Cross and get right with Him — not for forgiveness, since I am forgiven forever, but for sweet fellowship with Him and for power in His service.

Would you carefully examine yourself for "spots" of sin? I suggest you go over the following checklist thoughtfully then go back over it, repeating the process thoroughly several times until your sins are revealed one by one:

Ingratitude: For what blessing, or answered prayer, have you neglected to thank God?

Neglect of Bible reading: How many days have you gone without opening your Bible? How many days have you read it yet cannot remember what you have read?

Unbelief: What promise has God given that you doubt will be fulfilled? Are you doubting that He is willing to forgive any and all of your sin?

Prayerlessness: How often are your prayers just spiritual "chatter" — offered without fervent or focused faith? And remember, daydreaming or fantasizing is not prayer.

Unconcern for the lost: Who do you know who has never received Christ as Savior? When have you shared the gospel with that person? Never?

Ignorance of the lost: Did you skip church when a missionary was scheduled to speak because you thought he or she would be boring? Can you even name one missionary who is on your prayer list?

Hypocrisy: Are you pretending to be more spiritual than you are? Are you pretending to be anything that you are not?

Pride: Are you impressed with your own reputation and accomplishments? Are you offended and resentful when someone else receives attention? When sitting in church, instead of preparing your heart for worship, are you wondering if people have noticed your appearance?

Neglect of family: What have you truly sacrificed for their spiritual, physical, and emotional well-being? Nothing? Very little?

Neglect of God's family: Who has fallen into sin or disgrace within your church? What have you done to reach out to that person in love? Or is there someone within your church family who has lost a job or is in some physical or practical need, and you have said glibly, "I'm praying for you," yet have done nothing to help? And then did you quickly forget, and didn't pray?!

Envy: Who seems more gifted and fruitful and recognizable than you? Have you felt jealous?

Critical spirit: When have you found fault with someone because he or she doesn't measure up to your standards?

Slander: When have you told the truth about someone, with the intention of causing others to think less of him or her?

Lying: When have you either made a statement or tried to make an inference that was contrary to the unvarnished truth?

Cheating: When have you not done to others what you would have them do to you?

Robbing God: When have you exercised your gifts or spent your time, money, or energy on things that had a selfish goal, without asking God first?

The list goes on: *anger ... jealousy ... gossip ... worry ... doubt ... immorality* of any kind whether visual, mental, virtual, or actual ... [14]

It's a staggering indictment, isn't it? Go back over the list two or three times. Write down the sins in your own words, as they have been committed in your own life. Then add to all these sins the fact that knowing the good you *ought* to do and yet *don't* do, is also sin.[15] How many times have I *known* to get up early in the morning, slip out of my bed and onto my knees in order to begin my day in prayer, yet instead have rolled over and gone back to sleep?

That's sin for me.

As I meditate on what sin is, asking God to give me eyes to see myself in the light of who He is, the spots of sin in my life become a nightmare of guilt that rends my heart and leaves me totally humiliated, helpless, and hopeless. *And I'm in ministry!* The thought is appalling! How can I instruct others when I myself am responsible for sin and ruined by it? The turmoil in my heart and mind brought on by repeated failure wrenches from my lips an echo of Isaiah's outburst, "Woe to me!"

The pain is unbearable. The grief is all-consuming. When my heart is rended and I acknowledge what I've done that has hurt the very One who has given Himself for me, it would be so easy to dissolve into help-less self-pity and sink into hopeless ruin. But praise God! *Praise God!*

The very same thing that God used to save Isaiah He has used to save me ... and can use to save you from emotional, spiritual, and eternal misery and ruin.

But the way up, out of the miry pit of despair and depression, is down ... on our knees.

FIVE

Bend Your Knees!

Isaiah 6:6–7

The way up . . . is down.

Carole's Story

I'd like to say that in one sleepless night I confessed the pride in my life, woke up the next morning fully revived, and immediately began serving the Lord. It's true that in that one evening I did see the Lord's glory like never before. And in that evening, I was convicted of the overriding sin in my life. But it took weeks of prayer and ongoing confession, with the Holy Spirit shining that light into all the prideful crevices of my life, before I experienced full revival.

The best way to describe those prayerful months is by equating them to the night when the lower level of my home flooded with sewer water. Torrential rains had overwhelmed my city. When the deluge came, I quickly plugged my drains to keep more water from gushing in. But then I had to spend all night scooping out sewer water that had flowed into my downstairs rooms. Hour after hour, I carried bucket after bucket of murky slime up the steps and through my garage to empty the bucket onto my lawn that sloped away from the house. I felt like I was trying to empty an ocean one bucket at a time.

Early the next morning, after I had gotten all the water cleared and the rains had stopped, I remember taking out one of the last bucketfuls. As the overhead garage door rolled up, I saw the sun that was just beginning to rise into the clear, morning sky. This was the same sun I had seen on a pre-dawn run just the day before and thought to myself, Hmmm, nice sunrise. *But, this morning, it was as if I had never seen a sunrise before. The slogging in the sewer was over. It was a bright, shining, new day!*

Similarly, for several months, the Holy Spirit and I carried what seemed like bucket after bucket of prideful thoughts, motives, and actions out of the depths of my day-to-day life. Sometimes the bucket would fill during my morning devotions when I would pray, "Lord, show me where the pride is," and He'd lead me to a passage of Scripture that told me to rid something from my life. Sometimes it would fill at work when I'd realize I was going after a project because I wanted to be seen as one who was achieving. That was pride that had to be rooted out. Once it was on a long training run when I realized one of my motivations for running marathons was that I liked being able to say I had run twenty-six miles. More pride.

One bucket at a time, it got easier every day to recognize it and dump it from my life.

I didn't realize just how much had been cleaned out of my life until weeks later when I sat, again, in the audience of a Just Give Me Jesus *Revival. At the end of the message, Anne challenged each one in the audience to surrender whatever was keeping her from giving full adoration and service to the Lord. In that moment, because of all the pride that recently had been dredged from my life, I found myself standing, almost springing, to my feet waving my white flag of surrender. It was as if it were just me and the Lord, and in a voice both He and I heard, my heart spoke: "I know what it is, Lord. To You, this day, I surrender ... my career."*

It was in that moment, standing before the Lord, free from the sin that had previously ensnared me, that I knew what it was to be finally, fully revived ...

༄༅

Feeling Bad Never Felt So Good

Just when Isaiah was spiraling into the dark night of deep, despondent despair ... just when he surely thought he had plummeted as far into the pit of abandonment as anyone could go, things got even worse: "Then one of the seraphs flew to me with a live coal in his hand, which he had taken with tongs from the altar. With it he touched my mouth" (Isaiah 6:6 – 7).

As the live coal was pressed to Isaiah's lips, the searing pain must have been agonizing. Yet with the agonizing blisters would come the joy of sins forgiven and guilt atoned. For even as his lips were seared, the angel's words must have felt like a soothing balm to his tortured soul: "See, this has touched your lips; your guilt is taken away and your sin atoned for" (6:7).

Convicted ... Then Cleansed

From that moment on, Isaiah's life was never the same. I expect that with his lips that had been purified by holy fire, he never again

talked the same way ...

or thought the same way ...

or felt the same way ...

or looked the same way ...

or acted the same way ...

or walked the same way ...

or listened the same way ...

or lived the same way!

Praise God! There is hope for ruined sinners like Isaiah! For me! And for you! The hope is found, not in a burning coal of fire, but in what it represents — the blood of Jesus shed on the altar of the Cross[1] and applied ...

> to our lips and what we say,
> > to our ears and what we hear,
> > > to our minds and what we think,
> > > > to our eyes and what we see,
> > > > > to our hands and what we do,
> > > > > > to our feet and where we go,
> > > > > > > to our hearts and how we feel,
> > > > > > > > to our wills and what we decide.

My own searing conviction and confession of sin have left me feeling desperate for cleansing. I have longed to hear the same words of reassurance Isaiah heard. *And I have!* "Anne, the blood of Jesus, My Son, purifies you from every sin — past, present and even future sin.[2] ... Because you have confessed your sin, I will be faithful and just to forgive you and purify you from all unrighteousness.[3] ... Though your sins are like scarlet, they shall be as white as snow[4] ... As far as the east is from the west, so far have I removed your transgressions from you."[5]

This promise comes to mind from time to time as I work on my computer, because sometimes there are files or folders I want to throw away. In order to discard them, I have to drag them to the trash can on my screen. Then I hit the delete button. A little window pops up and asks if I'm sure I want to delete the trash, and when I affirm that I do by hitting the button a second time, the trash disappears. Totally. Permanently. I can't retrieve it, even if I try.

When you and I confess our sin and come to the Cross, we are cleansed with the blood of Jesus. It's as though God drags our sin to the heavenly trash can, hits the delete button, and it's gone! As far as the east is from the west, it's been removed. And if you think about it, the east is as far removed from the west as it's possible to be, since the two will never meet!

It's been said that there is only one thing God cannot do, and that is to remember your sin and mine that has been forgiven. When I come to Him humbly, through faith in Jesus, He erases my sin from His memory much more effectively than I erase things from my computer. Even Satan can't retrieve it from the inner workings of my spiritual hard drive![6]

Corrie ten Boom, author of *The Hiding Place* and survivor of the Nazi concentration camps during World War II, once remarked that God has cast our sins into the depths of the sea and posted a sign that says, "No Fishing Allowed."[7]

Every day, I bow in utter humility with a contrite heart that is filled with gratitude for the merciful, saving power of God, knowing with deep conviction that if He uses me in ministry it is purely by His grace alone. Because I'm just a desperate sinner, ruined and responsible for sin, but one who has been to the foot of the Cross, where the ground is level. No one — not the apostle Paul ... or Peter ... or Mary, the mother of Jesus ... or Mother Teresa ... or Pope John-Paul ... or Billy Graham — no one is exempt from the need to come to the Cross and be cleansed of sin. The level ground at the foot of the Cross leaves no room for . . .

self-righteousness

or judgmentalness

or a critical spirit

or pride

or self-promotion

or hypocrisy.

We are all helpless and hopeless in our sinful condition apart from the shed blood of Jesus Christ. So come with me now to the Cross.[8] Thank God for the blood of Jesus that has not lost its power to cleanse us of our sin. *All of it.*

Crucified ... Then Revived

Exposed in the light of Christ's holiness, with his lips blistered by the burning coal, I wonder if Isaiah had an experience of spiritual revival in much the same way as the apostle Paul, who years later would write, "I have been crucified with Christ and I no longer live, but Christ lives in me. The life I live in the body, I live by faith in the Son of God, who loved me and gave himself for me."[9] And were Isaiah's and Paul's experiences similar to that of the apostle John, in exile on Patmos, who, when his eyes were opened to the vision of the glory of Jesus Christ, "fell at his feet as though dead"?[10]

To fall at the feet of Jesus "as though dead" means primarily three things:

A dead man is silent — I've never heard a dead man speak.

A dead man is still — I've never seen a dead man move.

A dead man is totally surrendered — I've never known a dead man to think.

As a "dead" man, the apostle John was silent. He was no longer arguing with God's plan for his life, or making excuses for his sin, or telling God what he wanted Him to do, or rationalizing his behavior or insisting on his own way. And as a "dead" man he was still — no longer wrestling against God's will for his life, or going off in his own direction when God was going in a different direction, or impatiently running ahead of God. John was describing his "crucifixion" — total death to himself ...

to his rights,

to his wants,

to his dreams,

to his plans,

to his goals,

to his agendas,

to his own knowledge,

to his own wisdom,

to his own understanding,

to his own position,

to his own reputation.

And he was replacing those attributes with a deliberate, whole-hearted, unreserved devotion to God Himself. John was wholly surrendered, prostrate at the feet of Jesus, and content to lie there in rapt adoration and worship. In that moment and in that humble, selfless position he showed us that *the key to personal revival is the Cross — repentance of sin and death to self.*

In the silence and stillness, bathed in the light of the glory of Christ in an atmosphere that must have pulsated with His love, surely John's heart began to beat in sync with a divine rhythm. He must have been consumed with an intense compulsion to serve the One whom his eyes had seen and his ears had heard, because "then He placed His right hand on me and said: ... '*Write.*'"[11] And John did. The Revelation of Jesus Christ, that mysterious and thrilling glimpse into the throne room of heaven and the future of planet earth, is his eyewitness testimony recorded in passionate obedience to his Lord's command. But he could write it *only after* he had experienced personal revival through a fresh experience of the Cross.

Likewise, as Isaiah bowed in the flickering light of the burning coals, having repented of his sin and returned to the Cross, his heart also must have begun to beat in sync with that same divine rhythm. His entire being also must have been wholly captivated by the compelling desire to serve the One whose grace and mercy had been extended to him at the altar. And in that moment, Isaiah knew his life would never be the same ...

A genuine experience of personal revival resulting from a fresh encounter with Jesus is not a fleeting thing. It is not just educational. Or inspirational. Or motivational. Or emotional. It is life-changing. It truly is like waking up in our personal relationship with God so that now our lives entirely revolve around our passionate love for Jesus. You'll know your heart's been set aflame by the fire of revival when nothing else matters to you as much as He does — and your love for Him.

Called ... Then Set on Fire

Several years ago, my mother was just beginning to struggle with cataracts. To help herself read, she took from my father's desk a large magnifying glass that was connected to a swing arm with a clip at the end. She attached it to the arm of her floral, overstuffed easy chair by the window in her bedroom. As a voracious, insatiable reader, she found great delight in being able once again to immerse herself in her beloved books.

One beautiful morning, after reading for a while, Mother went to the kitchen at the opposite end of their long, stretched-out, log-cabin home. When she returned to her bedroom, she was amazed to find a tendril of smoke rising from the arm of her chair! When she investigated, she found that the sun pouring through the window had filtered through the magnifying glass, intensifying the light onto the upholstery until it had caught fire!

When Isaiah saw the Lord, the brilliance of the light — the purity and holiness and glory of who Jesus is — shone into Isaiah's heart with such intensity that it caught fire! His heart, mind, and soul were ignited with passionate love for Jesus. Then, in the pregnant pause that followed the burning coal being pressed to Isaiah's lips and with the angel's words still echoing in the air — *"your guilt is taken away and your sin atoned for"* — he experienced personal revival! From that moment on, his entire life was plunged into the intimacy of an all-consuming, personal relationship with the living God. From that moment on, nothing mattered more.

That same revival fire of intensity was ignited in John, the son of Zebedee and brother of James. He was an ordinary fisherman from Galilee with the nickname Son of Thunder, because he had such a fiery, explosive temper.[12] This same John, the brother of James, the son of Zebedee, and the Son of Thunder, was called by Jesus to be a disciple.[13] For three years, John personally observed Jesus walk on water, feed five thousand people with five loaves and two fish, create sight in a man born blind, cast evil spirits out with just a word, cleanse the lepers, and raise the dead! John knew Jesus, believed in Jesus, and followed Jesus — he was called — yet it wasn't until after Pentecost and an experience of personal revival that his life was radically changed and his heart was set on fire.

John would always be the son of Zebedee and brother of James, but following revival, he was no longer an ordinary fisherman. There would never be anything ordinary about him again, because his heart had been set on fire! His fearless preaching was validated by the miracle of changed lives,[14] and the powerful biography of Jesus that bears his name has continued to change lives for more than two thousand years.[15] Amazingly, instead of being nicknamed the Son of Thunder for his fiery temper, he is known today as the Apostle of Love because of the gentle tone of his writings.[16] And his eyewitness account of the end of human history has frightened and thrilled, puzzled and encouraged believers throughout the ages as it has given resounding hope to the hopeless.[17]

Overcoming persecution and exile with "patient endurance,"[18] John became an evangelist to the world, a best-selling author, and an incredibly effective church-planter and pastor. With courage that never faltered, he boldly proclaimed to a very pluralistic culture, "For God so loved the world that he gave his one and only Son, that whoever believes in him shall not perish but have eternal life."[19]

Are you thinking that obviously the apostle John was called to be a disciple, but not you? Do you think that only preachers, missionaries, and professional, full-time ministry people are called? Actually,

   if you've been saved …

   if you've been born again …

  if you've received Christ by faith as your Savior and Lord …

  if you're an authentic child of God …

then you've been called to be a disciple! You can't claim Jesus as Savior without accepting Him as Lord. He *is* Lord, and He commands that you and I follow Him in a life-long, moment-by-moment, surrendered obedience that we call discipleship.[20] The thrilling prospect is that when you are convicted … then cleansed, crucified … then revived, you are also called … then set on fire!

Can such life-changing, life-enriching, life-deepening revival really happen today? That question came to mind when I had lunch with an old friend. Thomas sat across the table from me.[21] He was a tall, trim, middle-aged man with graying hair and beard who had received Christ as his Savior when he was a boy. He had been raised in a Christian home and for years had been in ministry. But he described the impact of a recent encounter he had had with God this way:

"Anne, all my life I have believed in God, but now I *know* Him. I knew Jesus, but now He's real. His presence is more tangible to me than the chair I'm sitting in. I find myself praying all the time. I just can't seem to pray enough. And when I'm not praying, I'm reading my Bible. While driving my car, I just break out in songs of praise. He's alive in me, and I know it. I've never had so much joy!

"And Anne, I'm not afraid anymore. I'm not afraid of dying. I'm not afraid of living. I'm not afraid of hell. I'm not afraid of the devil. I'm not afraid of failure. I'm not afraid of the opinions of other people. I'm not afraid of my past, not afraid the skeletons will fall out of my closet. I'm not afraid to face the uncertainty of the future. I'm just not afraid. I have perfect peace!"

Thomas had experienced personal revival, and his life had changed — just as Isaiah's life changed after he had seen the Lord. Isaiah experienced personal revival, and it made a difference that lasted a lifetime — a difference that was immediately evident.

Previously Isaiah had thundered again and again, "Hear the word of the LORD," ... "Listen to the law of our God," ... "For the mouth of the LORD has spoken," ... "Therefore the Lord, the LORD Almighty, declares ..."

But *after* his revival, his preaching would bear witness that he had internalized God's Word, letting it penetrate his heart before he gave it out to others. *After* he had seen the Lord, his messages flowed, not from his head and his intellectual knowledge of God, but from his heart and his personal relationship with Him:

> "Then the LORD said *to Isaiah*"
>> — and he gave out God's Word.
>
> "The LORD said *to me*"
>> — and he gave out God's Word.
>
> "The LORD spoke *to me* again"
>> — and he gave out God's Word.

"The LORD spoke *to me* with his strong hand upon me"
— and He gave out God's Word.[22]

His words would glow with holy fire ignited by his sincere, heartfelt repentance and his return to the Cross.

It was at the foot of the Cross, with a body, soul, mind, and heart that must still have been quivering from the aftershock of seeing the Lord, that Isaiah's ears were opened and his heart was stirred as never before — *and he stepped out into greatness ...*

SIX

Just Say Yes!

Isaiah 6:8

Reject low living, sight walking, small planning,
casual praying, and limited giving —
God has chosen you for greatness.

Carole's Story

In my moment of "surrendering all," I'll be honest: I hadn't consciously thought that surrendering my career might mean actually quitting my job. But I know I meant my surrender with my whole heart. In hindsight, I know the Lord knew how genuine it was—more than I even realized myself.

A portion of Jeremiah 18 took on new meaning for me at that point in my life, the passage describing the potter and the clay. The New Living Translation says the potter made a jar that "did not turn out as he had hoped, so the potter squashed the jar into a lump of clay and started again" (v.4).

The Lord took me at my word that I wanted Him to have my entire life. Thankfully, He didn't just leave me on the wheel, fix me up by rounding off a few edges, and send me off to live my old life a little better. He gave me a whole new start in serving Him.

The Potter never changed, but you could say that I'm an entirely different pot. He squashed me and reshaped me. One day, within months of when I had stood in surrender, the phone in my office rang. To my surprise, on the other end of the line was Anne Graham Lotz, asking me to join the staff of her ministry as a revival director. In my heart I had been expecting a phone call—I had thought God might ask me to head up the Sunday school department or lead a Bible study in my home. But His plan for my life was so much more. Never in my wildest imagination could I have guessed that it would include a proposal to leave everything and go into full-time ministry. But in my conversation with Anne, I heard more than a job offer. I heard the voice of God calling me into service.

In a move that would have seemed absurd to me a year earlier, I left my twenty-year career, moved two thousand miles from home, and joined the full-time staff of her AnGeL Ministries ...

⌣⁚∾

Listen for His Voice

Learning to listen to God's voice is critical if you and I want to maintain the fire of our personal revival. Jesus taught that listening to His voice is one of the fundamental principles of discipleship. He described Himself as the Good Shepherd and you and me as His sheep when He taught, "The sheep listen to his [the Shepherd's] voice. He calls his own sheep by name and leads them out.... His sheep follow him because they know his voice."[1]

In Western civilization, the concept of a personal shepherd is relatively meaningless. When an epidemic of hoof-and-mouth disease was reported in the news a few years ago, we saw sheep ranches flashed on the news and sheep pens pictured on the front page of our morning newspapers, making the public aware of a little-noticed but vital industry. Sheep today graze in carefully fenced-in pastures and are guarded by specially bred dogs and identified by a number tattooed in their ears. Computers track when they are born and when they are ready for either shearing or slaughter. There is no personal shepherd. Unless the sheep are on a very small farm, even their owner can't tell one sheep from another.

But the Eastern shepherd was, and in many parts of the world still is, very different. He raised his sheep from the time they were lambs and maintained responsibility for them twenty-four hours a day, seven days a week, year in and year out, for their entire lifetime. There were no dogs or fences or tattoos or computers.

The Eastern shepherd of Jesus' day raised his sheep primarily in the Judean uplands. The countryside was rocky, hilly, and filled with deep crevices and ravines. Patches of grass were sparse. So the shepherd had to establish a personal, working relationship with each sheep, developing its love and trust in him in order to lead it to where the path was the smoothest, the pasture was the greenest, the water was the cleanest, and the nights were the safest. The shepherd always *led* the sheep. He knew their names, and when he called them, they recognized his voice, following him like a swarm of little chicks follows the mother hen. When he stopped, the sheep huddled closely around him, pressing against his legs. Their personal relationship with him was based on his voice, which they knew and trusted.

In this parable, you and I are the sheep, the Good Shepherd is Jesus, and the voice of the Good Shepherd is the Word of God. Our Shepherd speaks to us through the written words of our Bible, and His words are personal.

His Words Are Personal

Several years ago, to celebrate my father's eighty-second birthday, President George W. Bush invited Daddy and members of the immediate family, along with special friends, to the White House for dinner. It was my privilege to be included on that very special occasion. I was seated at a round table that included my father, Mrs. Bush, Steve Case, Cliff Barrows, my brother Ned, and others. In friendly conversation, my father related a story to the entire table. Everyone at the table knew he was speaking to them. But then he turned, looked straight at me, and said, "Anne ...," and I knew he was speaking *personally* to me.

When I open my Bible, I know God is speaking to me because God speaks to everyone through His Word. But there are times when I open my Bible and a verse or a passage seems to leap up off the page with my name on it. Then I know God is speaking to me, personally. This happened recently when I was conducting *A Passionate Pursuit*.

A Passionate Pursuit is my ministry's breakaway retreat/seminar for women that is designed to take them deeper into God's Word and equip them to lead others into it, while also helping them maintain the fire of revival in their hearts. The three days of teaching are intense; they tax me to the limits of my spiritual, physical, emotional, and mental abilities. This past year, in the days immediately preceding *A Passionate Pursuit*, I came down with my third case of pneumonia-type flu. I went to the host city while taking antibiotics along with fistfuls of vitamin C and echinacea. After almost three decades of teaching, I knew God would be faithful to see me through, but I still felt *so sick and tired ...*

The morning of the first day of the breakaway, I opened the *Daily Light*, a volume of selected Scriptures I have read every day of my life since I was ten years old. Here is the way I "heard" those Scriptures that morning:

" 'Be strong ... and work; for I am with you, Anne,' says the LORD of hosts."

Lord, You mean I can do all things through Christ who strengthens me?

"Yes, Anne, [Be] strong in the Lord and in the power of His might.... The joy of the LORD is your strength.... The LORD turned to Anne and said, 'Go in this might of yours....' If God is for you, Anne, who can be against you?... Therefore, Anne, you have received mercy, so do not lose heart.... Don't grow weary while doing good, for in due season you will reap if you do not lose heart."

Thank You, Thank You. ... Thanks be to God, who gives me the victory through our Lord Jesus Christ.[2]

As I read those verses, I clearly and distinctly heard my Shepherd speaking to me with a heart filled with compassion, sensitive to the challenge that was facing me and with genuine understanding of my weakness. I was so encouraged and strengthened by His words that I was enabled to carry out my assignment triumphantly. None of the women who came to the breakaway ever suspected how I had struggled.

When our Shepherd speaks, He speaks to us personally — by name. He knows us inside and out.

> He knows our thoughts before they're on our minds,
> and our words before they're even formed on our tongues,
> and our emotions before they're felt in our hearts,
> and our actions before there is any movement.

He speaks in the language of our own personal lives.

When have you heard the voice of your Shepherd speaking to you? When have you heard Him calling you by name? When you read your Bible, do you just focus on the facts and information, the commands and the promises, the warnings and the encouragement, the examples and the exhortations? *When have your ears been opened to His voice within the pages, calling you by name...?*

His Words Flow from His Heart

Isaiah's ears were opened to the voice of God when his knowledge and relationship with God dropped the eighteen inches from his head to his heart. *When* he was drawn into close, intimate fellowship with the One who was his Creator, his Redeemer, and his King — the One who was seated on the throne, high and exalted — it was *then* that he heard the voice of God, saying, "Whom shall I send? And who will go for us?" (6:8). It was *then* that Isaiah's ears were opened to the cry of God's heart!

That same, specific cry was echoed years later, after Jesus had met with the sinful Samaritan woman beside Jacob's well on a hot, dusty day in Sychar. When His disciples brought to Him the food they had found in town, they insisted that He eat. Their words conveyed a hidden sense of urgency to continue their journey so they could distance themselves from the despised Samaritans as quickly as possible.

But instead of opening His mouth to satisfy His physical hunger, Jesus cried out with a broken heart for a lost world. In a voice that surely pulsated with that same divine rhythm that was in sync with the heart of His Father, He commanded, "Open your eyes and look at the fields! ... The harvest is plentiful, but the workers are few. Ask the Lord of the harvest, therefore, to send out workers into his harvest field. Go! I am sending you."[3]

That motley band of fishermen, tax collectors, and ordinary men must have stared at Him like He had lost His mind: "Who, *me?* Go *where?* To Jerusalem and the *Jews?* To the Samaritans and the *outcasts?* To Judea and the *religious?* To the whole world — *secularist, atheist, pagan, humanist?*"

The thrilling truth for you and me to contemplate is that after the disciples had been to the Cross, had a personal encounter with the risen Christ, and experienced the explosive power of personal revival at Pentecost, *they did go!* They took the gospel of Jesus Christ to the whole world! Almost two thousand years later, I am the fruit of their faithful obedience that flowed from their personal revival!

That same heart cry of God has reverberated throughout the ages, ever since Jesus articulated it to His disciples on a mountainside in Galilee: "Therefore go and make disciples of all nations, baptizing them in the name of the Father and of the Son and of the Holy Spirit, and teaching them to obey everything I have commanded you. And surely I am with you always, to the very end of the age."[4]

When have *you* heard that heart cry?

His Words Are Directed ... to You

Isaiah overheard the Lord's cry — "Whom shall I send? And who will go for us?"

Like you and me, Isaiah could have looked around to see who the Lord was speaking to. He could have searched for someone to go. He could have wept pitifully for a lost and broken world. He could have desperately prayed that God would send workers into the fields. He could have wished that surely *someone else* would answer the call.

After God's cry rang out, I wonder if there were several moments of quiet. Dead silence while nothing moved. No one appeared to come forward. God's cry must have hung heavy in the air ... waiting ...

Others might have worried, Oh no, God! You don't mean me!

Some, like Moses, might have begged, "O Lord, please send someone else to do it."[5] (Or, as some pundits have put Moses' attempted hand-off to his brother, "Here am I — send Aaron!")

Most of us might have thought, *Not me! You surely don't mean me! I know there's a missionary around here somewhere. There's got to be! Or an evangelist! Someone who really is called — you know, with hand-writing on the wall and everything. Going into all the world and making disciples is for other people. I'll pray, and I'll even give money, but surely you don't mean for me to go? Me?!*

That's the way I have responded in the past: "Lord,

I'm too young.

I'm too old.

I'm too busy.

I'm not educated enough.

I'm not wealthy enough.

I'm not smart enough.

I'm not spiritual enough.

I'm not healthy enough.

Surely you don't mean me! Not *me*!"

But that was *before* personal revival. That was before I saw the LORD. Now my greatest fear is that He won't call me into service or that if He does, somehow I won't hear Him.

Isaiah not only listened to God's voice, he also applied to himself what God said. This is all the more amazing when you realize that, at this turning point in Isaiah's life, God wasn't speaking directly to him. There was no handwriting on the wall, no lightning bolt from the sky, not even a direct call. At this strategic moment, Isaiah *overheard* God speaking, as though He was talking to anyone who would choose to listen.

When you and I open our Bibles, God is speaking . . . to anyone who has the ears to hear His voice. But how many people who read and even hear Him speak actually *apply* what He says to their own lives?

Isaiah did. Isaiah must have timidly spoken up in a hushed voice that faltered with humble contrition yet was resolutely empowered by the rhythm of that divine heartbeat, "Here am I. Send me!" (6:8): *Here I am Lord. You remember me. I'm the one who, when my life was shaken by King Uzziah's death, had my eyes opened in a fresh way to Your holi-*

ness. And in the light of who You are, I have seen myself and my service and my sin in a radically devastating way. I'm acutely aware that I am utterly helpless in myself to ever live for You or serve You in a way that would please You or would make any eternal difference to anyone. But, dear God, I've been to the Cross! My guilt has been taken away and my sin atoned for! And oh, God! If You could ever use me, here I am! It would be the highest privilege of my life to do something for the One who has done so much for me. Please, dear God, call me into service. Send me!

Or, to put Isaiah's response more simply and briefly, "Yes, Lord. Yes! Yes Sir!"

God said, "Go" (6:9). And Isaiah went. And so have I.

One of the lasting impacts of personal revival is that it has made a difference in my life. I not only listen to the voice of Jesus and apply His words to my life, but I live for Him alone. I am so caught up in who He is and what He has done for me that I no longer consider my life my own. My life is laid down at His nail-pierced feet, totally available for His use. Anytime. Anywhere. Anyway. The supreme joy of my life is to be available to Him.

Are you thinking, *Well, that sounds fine for you, Anne, but I'm not so sure . . . ?* Are you hesitating because you're not sure such a commitment is worth it? Are you wondering what you will get out of it? Then let me share with you what *I* have gotten out of it. Personal revival has given me more of . . .

> His consistency in my devotion,
> His fervency in my prayers,
> His simplicity in my lifestyle,
> His humility in my attitude,
> His purity in my motives,

His faithfulness in my commitments,
His unselfishness in my relationships,
His forgiveness in my conflicts,
His gentleness in my actions,
His kindness in my marriage.

His blessings in my brokenness,
His strength in my weakness,
His courage in my convictions,
His joy in my circumstances,
His will in my priorities.

His contentment in my disappointments,
His wisdom in my decisions,
His discipline in my day,
His vision in my dreams.

His purpose in my steps,
His peace in my storms,
His presence in my home,
His power in my life.

His tears in my eyes,
His voice in my ears,
His thoughts in my mind,
His work in my hands,
His words in my mouth,
His love in my heart.

The glorious blessing I have received as a result of answering the call to personal revival is that . . .

in me,

with me,

around me,

before me,

behind me,

below me,

above me . . .

I've been saturated with more of . . . JESUS!

What are you waiting for? Wake up! Sometimes God rends your heart to open it up and make room for the world. So get moving! *A wake-up call is a call to action . . .*

SEVEN

Move Your Feet!

Isaiah 6:9 – 13

Now your life has purpose and eternal significance.

Carole's Story

Instead of reaching up to grasp the top rung of the corporate ladder, I've spent the past five years reaching out, in Christ's name, to the church in America and all over the world. In a plan only the Lord could have devised for my life, I get to use the experience and training gained in my corporate years to tend to the administrative aspects of a ministry that reaches thousands of people on every continent with the Word of God. It's like the Lord took my love of technology, my bent toward administration, and redirected it for His purpose, not Carole's.

The biggest goal I could have ever set for myself, the highest aspiration I could have ever had in my pre-revival, secular career, could never touch what I've experienced in my heart and in my service since I received a fresh touch—and a new assignment—from Him.

I gave Him my whole life, and He gave me a whole new purpose. When I took my eyes off myself, He showed me an entire world—through His.

In the same way I couldn't have told you before that November 2000 night that I was in need of revival, I can tell you now that I definitely couldn't have imagined I would be serving Him in full-time ministry. In His grace and mercy, He not only accepted my broken and contrite heart, He gave me a gift—a fresh touch from Himself. I gave Him my whole life, and He gave me a whole new purpose.

Revival, for me, isn't about leaving behind what the world had to offer. It's about leaving behind sin so that I can embrace the richer life the Lord has to offer ...

~:~

Just Do It

Several years ago, Nike ran a television advertisement that remains one of my all-time favorites. The ad pictured Michael Jordan, the greatest basketball player who has ever played the game, dribbling a basketball down the court. When he approached the foul line, he just seemed to take off into the air. With his long legs spread-eagled, his tongue curling out of his mouth, sweat flying from his bald head, brown fingers wrapped around the basketball, arm poised in a graceful arc above his head, and eyes intently focused on the goal, he actually seemed to fly! His flight took him above the rim of the basketball goal — then he swiftly brought his arm down and jammed the ball through the net. At this point, the television screen went black, and three words appeared: Just Do It!

The message was clear. There came a time for Michael Jordan to stop bragging and talking and planning and thinking and practicing and dribbling ... and *just do it!* Just put the ball in the basket!

In the same way, there comes a time for Christians — for you and me — to stop reading and studying and discussing and thinking and praying and repenting ... and just do it! Put all that you know and all you've experienced into practice and start living it out. Now. The time has come for you to move your feet.

Along with Isaiah, the prophet Ezekiel has been something of a role model for me as he has challenged me to respond to my own vision of the Lord, not with pious platitudes or super-spirituality, but with action ... and *just do it.* Just move out in service to the Lord. Ezekiel was an Israelite exiled in Babylon, living in a refugee camp on top of a garbage dump, who also could say, "I saw the Lord." He testified, "When I saw [Him], I fell face down, and I heard the voice of one speaking.... He said: 'Son of man, I am sending you.'"[1]

While personal revival is something to be cherished in our hearts forever ... while it is something to be scrupulously maintained ... while it is something that brings great joy and deep peace ... it is also something that should compel us to serve the One who has set us on fire! In fact, if it doesn't, I question its validity. You *cannot* experience personal revival in your relationship with Jesus Christ and *do nothing*!

If you truly have awakened, opened your eyes, rended your heart, bent your knees, and said yes, then it naturally follows that you must — it's not an option — you *must* move your feet! If you claim, "I've seen the Lord," what difference has it made? What difference has it made that others can see? *What impact has your vision of Jesus had on your life?*

Compelled by the Vision

The apostle Paul, breathing fire and brimstone, was headed for Damascus, clutching a document that gave him full authority to persecute Christians there. As he approached the city, a blindingly brilliant light shone from heaven. He fell on his face and heard a voice inquiring, "Why do you persecute me?" When he asked who was speaking, the voice replied, "I am Jesus, whom you are persecuting.... Now get up and stand on your feet.... I am sending you" out.[2] As Paul related his testimony when on trial before King Agrippa, he stated, "So then, King Agrippa, I was not disobedient to the vision from heaven."[3] In fact,

Paul, the chief persecutor of believers, became the greatest evangelist perhaps the world has ever known.

After the apostle John saw the Lord, he "fell at his feet as though dead," and later, as a direct result of the vision, he wrote the Revelation of Jesus Christ.[4]

> Because Isaiah had seen the Lord, he did something!
> He moved his feet as he lived for Jesus alone.
> Because Ezekiel had seen the Lord, he did something!
> He moved his feet as he lived for Jesus alone.
> Because Paul had seen the Lord, he did something!
> He moved his feet as he lived for Jesus alone.
> Because John had seen the Lord, he did something!
> He moved his feet as he lived for Jesus alone.

If you have seen the Lord, *what have you done?*

Why are you still standing there? *Who or what are you living for?*

This is your wake-up call! It's time to get up! It's time to suit up! It's time to answer God's call to personal revival by returning to the Cross, repenting of your sin, and moving your feet as you recommit yourself to live for Jesus, and Jesus alone. The vision is compelling! And so is your love . . .

Compelled by Your Love

When you love others, do you find it hard to sit still and do nothing for them when they're nearby? I do. My children, their spouses, and the grandchildren usually gather at our home on Sunday afternoons and evenings to play, visit, eat, watch a ball game, and just generally enjoy each other's company. When they come, I find myself constantly jumping up to get something, to help someone, to play games or cook supper or serve refreshments. Because I love them, I derive great pleasure in doing something for them.

Recently I was reminded of the way serving others expresses our love for them when I went home to visit my parents. For years and years, my parents have been very strong and self-sufficient. They have served and given and worked and ministered to others, as well as to me, as long as I can remember. My entire life, I have been the recipient of their loving actions and activities. Truly they have been an incredible blessing to me!

As my parents have grown older, they have become more and more physically inactive. Mother can no longer walk or see well. She can no longer cook meals or freshen my room or even stand at the door to greet me when I arrive. Daddy has difficulty keeping his balance when walking and has become quite deaf. He can no longer hike the mountain with me or talk on the telephone or even enter easily into conversation at the dinner table. They are fortunate to have a very able, willing staff that takes care of their practical needs.

While I mourn the loss of their physical strength and share their frustration over the fullness of inner life that is bound in the weakness of an outer body, I derive great joy and personal pleasure in being able, at long last, to do something for *them*. I love to bake them a homemade apple pie or fix a sumptuous pot roast with all the trimmings for Sunday lunch. I love to throw an extra log on the fire for Mother or run to get a requested book for Daddy. I love to tuck a lap robe around Mother's frail body or adjust Daddy's chair to just the right angle. I love to insert the video they want to watch into the machine and then find the right remote control to run it. I love to open the window so they can get some fresh air, then close it when they get chilled. I love doing those little things that say, *I love you!*

It stands to reason that we want to do something for those that we love. Do you love Jesus — *really love Him?* I do! And in my love for Him

I seem to hear Him whispering to my heart the same thing He said to Peter that day so long ago beside the Sea of Galilee ...

Peter had just had a dramatic, fresh encounter with Jesus. *Peter had seen the Lord!* The sun was rising in the morning sky, the fire was burning down, and the last morsels of fish and the last crumbs of bread had been consumed. Like the rest of us, Jesus loved His own, and He had just done something for them by fixing them breakfast. He then turned His full attention to Peter. Lovingly and patiently and persistently He challenged Peter, *If you love Me, do something for Me.*[5]

The apostle Paul's vision of the glory of the resurrected Jesus compelled him to immediately do something about what he had seen. He began telling people in Damascus about Jesus; then he proceeded to Jerusalem, Judea, and the rest of the known world of his day, proclaiming Jesus until he died! He just couldn't have an encounter with the living Lord Jesus Christ *and do nothing*! When writing to the Christians at Corinth, he said, "Christ's love compels us, because we are convinced that one died for all ... that those who live should no longer live for themselves but for him who died for them and was raised again."[6]

The work Jesus had for Peter to do was different than the work He had for Paul, a lesson underscoring the Scripture that tells us, "There are different kinds of service, but the same Lord."[7] The work He has for me will be different than the work He has for you.
Some of us preach,
> and some of us teach,
>> and some of us provide technical assistance with
>>> audio and video and computers.
Some of us keep the nursery,
> and some of us cook in the kitchen,
>> and some of us lead in worship.

Some of us write books,
    and some of us write music,
        and some of us give legal counsel to the poor.
Some of us visit the prisoner,
    and some of us greet church visitors,
        and some of us clean the sanctuary.
Some of us feed the hungry,
    and some of us house the homeless,
        and some of us care for the dying.

What we do for Jesus doesn't have to be something big. The important thing is how we do it. As Paul urged the Colossians, "Whatever you do, work at it with all your heart, as working for the Lord, not for men."[8] Carved into the frame of the window over my kitchen sink — the same thing that is carved into a sign over my mother's kitchen sink — is this reminder: DIVINE SERVICE WILL BE RENDERED HERE THREE TIMES DAILY. The words help me remember that feeding my family and serving them, when done as unto the Lord, is divine service.

Regardless of the divine service we find to do for Him, our mission is the same: to go into all the world and make disciples of all nations.[9] And that world, as author and Bible teacher Jill Briscoe has pointed out, is not necessarily Africa or Asia but the world between our own two feet. Our mission involves telling others who Jesus is and what He has done for them. When those we have prayed for and shared Christ with respond by placing their faith in Him as Lord and Savior, our mission expands to include helping them grow up in faith until they, in turn, can bring others to salvation and help them grow into disciples also — and on and on for generation after generation.[10]

In our work and in our mission we are motivated, not by a sense of duty, not by our pride or privileges, not by our reputations or responsibilities, but by the same revival fire that burned within Peter and

Paul: we have seen the Lord, and we work for Him simply because we love Him!

The same was true for Isaiah. Following his vision of the glory of the Lord, he humbly made himself available for service. Almost immediately, the assignment was given: "Go and tell this people ..." (6:9). His assignment was to relay the message God gave him to people who would "be ever hearing, but never understanding; be ever seeing, but never perceiving" (6:9). He was assigned to go to people who just would never get it! They would be totally unreceptive to the truth. But because he would continue to give them God's Word and they would continue to resist, he would "make the heart of this people calloused; make their ears dull" (6:10). They never would be healed because they never would repent of their sin. Isaiah was assigned a very tough task!

Who are the people the Lord is sending you to? Your family? Your neighbors? Your coworkers? Your business partner? Your church congregation? Your students? Your classmates? Your roommates?

Is He sending you to people in another city ... or state ... or country ... or continent? To people of another language ... or race ... or culture? Are you flinching or hesitating or procrastinating or resisting because it just seems *so hard*?

Sometimes I wonder if we, living in America in the twenty-first century, know what "hard" really is. During the 1890s, "Uncle" Jimmy Graham, as he was affectionately known, was sent by God to the people of China as a missionary with his wife, "Aunt" Sophie.[11] Joined by Absalom Sydenstricker, Pearl Buck's[12] father, he opened the mission station that my maternal grandparents joined in 1916. Uncle Jimmy studied and quickly caught onto the tonal language, then began to preach the gospel from village to village and town to town in Kiangsu Province. For more than eighteen months, he never had even one positive response to his message. Aunt Sophie said there was not a night when he came in that he was not covered in bruises from the rocks the peasants had hurled at him or when his face wasn't dripping with their spit.

Years later, my mother had opportunity to ask him if he ever got discouraged. She said he looked perplexed, as though he didn't know what that word meant. He responded, "No. No. The battle is the Lord's, and He will deliver it into our hand."

What hardship do you face as you go about your work for the Lord? Can it compare with the challenges faced by Uncle Jimmy Graham — or by Isaiah?

Compelled by His Command

In spite of the freshness of Isaiah's vision and the overflow of his heart and the sincerity of his offer — "Here am I. Send me!" — he couldn't help but blurt out, as he visualized the work ahead of him: "For how long, O Lord?" (6:11).

In other words, *I'm not sure I can do this. It sounds like it could be dangerous. At the least, this job will make me unpopular, and I'll probably lose any social standing I might otherwise have had. There can't be much money in this either, so I'll probably be poor. But the worst is that I can't imagine the heartache of pouring out my life to tell others about You and never having anyone respond positively or receive it personally or repent permanently. Maybe my gifts lie in other areas, Lord. Could I try it just for a little while ... ?*

There must have been a ringing sound of authority and finality to the Lord's voice as He responded to Isaiah's query, because He left no doubt as to how long Isaiah was to serve: "until the cities lie ruined and without inhabitant, until the houses are left deserted and the fields ruined and ravaged, until the LORD has sent everyone far away and the land is utterly forsaken" (6:11 – 12). Isaiah was commanded to serve until he no longer had any opportunity to do so — or until judgment came. His service was not to be some holy hobby or some short-term project … *it was to be a lifestyle!*

The success of Isaiah's service would not be determined by the number of people whose lives he changed but by his faithfulness to obey his Lord. In that obedience would come the deep sense of satisfaction and fulfillment and joy he longed for, rewards he would find as he lived his life to serve and please the One he loved.

Isaiah obeyed. Given his assignment and considering his devoted obedience to it, it's no wonder he became the greatest of the Old Testament prophets.

What assignment has God given you? Would you ask Him? I know He has one in mind for you because He told us clearly, through the words of the apostle Paul, that "we are God's workmanship, created in Christ Jesus to do good works, which God prepared in advance for us to do."[13]

Don't dodge your assignment because it seems to lack any chance for success. Don't miss your assignment because it seems such an insignificant, small thing.[14] The church in Europe was birthed when Paul spoke to a handful of women on a river bank.[15] The size and scope of the assignment are up to Him, and the effectiveness and lasting impact of your service are also His responsibility.[16] You and I are simply to be faithfully available … and obedient.

The assignments God has given me have taken me way beyond my comfort zone. While some of them have begun small and stayed small, others have begun small and grown larger, while still others were begun large and blossomed into major tasks.

There have been times when I have argued, resisted, procrastinated, and questioned, but in the end I always give in, because He is my Lord … I have "seen" Him … and I love Him. I don't serve Him because I have to. I serve Him because I want to do something for Him. And in the process of being obedient, I have come to know Him. He has "made known to me the path of life. He has filled me with joy in His presence, with eternal pleasures at His right hand."[17]

With eagerness and enthusiasm, I put my feet in motion. I want to serve Him all the days of my life. I want to stay awake to His glorious vision forever. I am now on a passionate pursuit for more of Jesus. I embrace the Cross that shatters the stranglehold of self and enlarges my capacity to receive more. I long . . .

to gaze on His visible face,

to hear His audible voice,

to feel His unmistakable touch,

to become an eyewitness of His glory.

In the meantime, I refuse to sleep one more minute. I'm awake . . . with eyes opened, heart rended, and knees bent while I whisper, "Yes . . . Yes, Lord! . . . *Yes Sir!*" then raise my hand as I move my feet. "I'm available for service. Send me. I'll go. *I want to stay awake forever . . .*"

EIGHT

Stay Awake!

Don't lose that lovin' feelin'.

Carole's Story

Maintaining the fire of revival in my life has required effort. My pride still seems to be the "water" that threatens to put out the fire within me. But the close-up look at the pride in my life when I saw the Lord has made it easier to recognize this specific sin when it makes its periodic attempts to return.

The year I woke up to find my career had replaced Jesus as my "first love," I repented of my sin and asked the Lord to help me never go back into it. He and I both knew I needed a divine anchor, something to grab at the first hint that my prideful self was resurfacing.

The anchor He gave me was His Word. In particular, the first eleven verses of Philippians 2. Like a magnet, I have been drawn to these words that describe genuine humility—Christ's humility. This passage is underlined and dated in every Bible I own. It's on a yellow sticky note on my bathroom mirror. It's written on the inside cover of my prayer journal. It's memorized in my brain. It's the log that helps to keep my fire burning.

More than once in the past five years ... I have wearily read through those eleven verses word by word in a stark hotel room in some foreign country ... I have prayed through them during my quiet time at home in the sometimes-lonely city where I've moved to work in full-time ministry ... I have recited them quietly to myself before returning a call to the headhunter who has offered me a high-paying job and the chance to get back on the career path I left. I have felt the Holy Spirit bring the passage to my mind to almost scold me whenever repentance is in order.

In other words, temptations and challenges have come and gone. But when I saw the Lord in a fresh way, He was quick to show me that keeping His Word central in my life was my only hope for never losing the freshness. It really works. His plan for my life is the only one I follow, and I pray I never see it any other way.

༈

Stir Up the Fire

Have you ever worked hard to build a fire, only to have it go out? Although I was raised in a log cabin with five fireplaces, I never learned to build a fire that would last. One of those fireplaces is in my mother's bedroom. When I go home, I invariably find her sitting in her over-stuffed chair by the window with a roaring fire on the hearth. As we sit and visit, the fire dies down, and she frequently reminds me to "stir up the fire, Anne," or "put another log on it."

You and I can respond to our wake-up call and experience the thrilling fire of personal revival, but if we neglect that fire, it will die out. And nothing is more miserable than a heart that has grown cold, chilling a life that once knew the raging warmth of a passionate relationship with Jesus. Not only does a heart that's grown cold make us miserable, but it makes Him miserable too. It grieves the Lord. Speaking to the Ephesian church through the apostle John, Jesus explained, "I know your deeds, your hard work and your perseverance.... You have persevered and have endured hardships for my name, and have not grown weary. Yet I hold this against you: You have forsaken your first love."[1]

Jesus loves you and me, and He longs to be loved — *really loved* — by us in return.

For twelve years I taught a weekly Bible class of five hundred women in our city. I never missed a class. During that time, through the disciplined study of His Word, God gave me a wonderful love for Jesus. At the end of those twelve years, I knew with absolute certainty God was calling me to leave the class and go into an itinerant, Bible-teaching ministry.

I left the class and went out into the world. Literally. Three months later I found myself in Fiji helping lead a conference of five hundred pastors who had come in from other islands for miles around. Five months later I was in Brazil leading another conference for approximately fifteen hundred pastors and evangelists from all over the country and squeezing in a youth conference of more than two thousand young people. In between Fiji and Brazil, I was teaching in seminars and conferences every week in the United States.

Gradually I became aware that I was having to drag myself into my quiet time, that my heart no longer seemed to be uplifted in worship, and that I didn't feel any real joy, but I thought I was just tired. I thought I must be suffering from prolonged jet lag along with time and food changes.

One morning, in my devotions, I read Revelation 2:1 – 7 and sensed, in my heart, Jesus speaking to me: "Anne, I *know* your deeds. I know all about Fiji and the extra sessions that were dumped on you that you accepted because of your commitment to Me. I know all about Brazil and the women's sessions you booked into your free time because of your heart to get others into My Word. I *know* your hard work and your perseverance. I *know* you have endured hardships in My name and have not grown weary. Thank you, Anne, for all you are doing to serve Me. Yet I hold this against you: you are losing your love for Me."

When I came to that verse, I kept on reading. I knew He couldn't be speaking to me! After all, I was traveling around the world telling others how to love Him! *Surely* He wasn't speaking to me!

But He was! He kept drawing my attention back to those verses until I finally listened to what He had to say. I would have denied it and vehemently argued, except it was *Jesus* who was speaking to me! And I knew that whenever He speaks, it's the truth. Finally, the light of His Word penetrated my delusion. Deep in my heart, I acknowledged that I wasn't just tired; I *was* losing my love for Him! I cannot tell you how devastatingly painful that revelation was to me. I yearned to love Him, and I thought I did. But He did not agree.

With tears streaming down my cheeks, I asked, "Lord, what would You have me do?"

He replied from Revelation 2:5. "Remember the height from which you have fallen."

Remember what it was like to love Me with all your heart, mind, soul, and strength.

I remembered. That love was the "height" in my relationship with Christ. And when I lost it, it was a long way down.

Then, still from verse 5, He said, "Repent."

Repentance means to stop it: stop going in one direction; turn around, and go in the opposite direction. Since a "first love" is an emotional, affectionate, passionate love, and because emotions really can't be controlled or dictated, I responded, "Lord, how? I want to repent of losing my first love for You, I want to stop not loving You emotionally and affectionately and passionately. But how? I am willing to repent, but I don't know how."

Again, He spoke to me from verse 5. "Return to the things you did at first."

And I answered, "What things? Things I did when I was first born again? Things I did when I first began to serve You?"

And He seemed to point out two "first things" I needed to return to.

Simply stated, the two things were the "logs" for the revival fire that I will describe in this chapter: daily, disciplined prayer and Bible reading. The fire in my heart was burning dangerously low because it didn't have enough fuel. Believe me, before that day was out, I had added those logs to my fire! And within a short time, it was rekindled into a roaring blaze.

Your fire will go out also if you neglect to stir it up and stop putting the logs on it.

So ... *stir up the fire!* Come along with me, and as we work through this last chapter together, I'll show you how. The two primary spiritual disciplines I will teach you in this chapter are designed to help you maintain the fire of revival in your life. Don't neglect them or ignore them, or the fire will go out! The Bible tells us to "fan into flame the gift of God."[2] That gift is the Holy Spirit, who is the fire of God, igniting our personal, permanent, passionate relationship with Jesus!

I've noticed that when I respond to my mother's request to "stir up the fire," when I poke it or turn over a log or blow on it, the fire will flare up briefly, but then it will die out if I don't add another log. And if I add one log, the fire ignites and burns nicely. But if I add two logs, the fire begins to crackle and blaze, and soon there's a raging fire that becomes a source of warmth and light for the entire room. In the same way, for personal revival to ignite, blaze, and even become a raging fire in your heart that lasts, affecting not only yourself but those around you, add not one but two logs to the fire ...

The First Log for the Revival Fire: Talk to Him

What kind of a year, or month, or week have you had? Has it been …

physically exhausting?

emotionally depleting?

spiritually draining?

socially depressing?

relationally devastating?

professionally discouraging?

financially challenging?

Do you long to just sit down and talk to someone about it? Someone who is a wise, caring, attentive listener? Someone with integrity, who can keep confidences? Someone who won't silently smirk at your stupidity or ignorance but will actually love you while patiently listening?

There are times my heart aches to have someone to talk to about me … and them … and it … and you. So I carve out time to get alone, curl up in my easy chair by the fire, and imagine Jesus sitting there in another chair opposite me. And I just talk to Him … that is the privilege we call prayer.

For the next few moments, let's talk to Him together. I'll guide you gently, using a pattern you can use in subsequent prayer times by yourself. The subheads that follow lead you through a pattern of prayer, and I hope you will pray with me through this entire section in one sitting so that you receive the richest blessing from our time together. I'll initiate the conversation to make it easier for you, but don't hesitate to "interrupt" me when you want to say something. And I'm going to tuck in the words of some familiar old hymns to help us articulate our thoughts.

We're going to begin with worship, which will lead us, as it led Isaiah, into confession of sin, a private exchange between you and

God. Following a time of confession, I think my heart would burst if I couldn't give voice to my praise for all He has done for me, so next we will thank Him together. Then we'll give voice to our requests for others and ourselves.

I never cease to be amazed that Jesus invites you and me, as His children and in His name . . .

> to come into His Father's presence,
> to crawl up into His lap by faith,
> to put our head on His shoulder of strength,
> to feel His loving arms of protection around us,
> and to pour out our hearts.

As God's only Son, Jesus took advantage of this same privilege of prayer. His heart also must have ached to talk to His heavenly Father. He too needed a loving listener, Someone He could trust with His innermost thoughts and feelings. Someone who would never betray or deny Him — which is one reason He prayed when there was no special reason to pray,[3] except that He simply wanted to talk. So He . . .

> prayed privately,
> prayed publicly,
> prayed alone,
> prayed with friends,
> prayed in crowds . . .
> prayed standing,
> prayed sitting,
> prayed kneeling,
> prayed on His face . . .
> prayed early in the morning,
> prayed late in the evening,
> prayed during the day,
> prayed all night.

Jesus prayed! He loved to talk to His Father.

I love to talk to Him too. That's what we'll do as we add this "log" to our revival fire.

Help Me Be Still

Do you ever get an opportunity to talk with someone you've just been dying to talk with, then when the time comes, you can't think of anything to say?

That has happened to me many, many times in prayer. It's amazing: how can I love God so much and long to talk with Him so much, yet be so tongue-tied in His presence? I wonder ... could that be a sign that I *am* in His presence? Is He inviting me just to be quiet for a few moments ... to simply be still, as the words of this beloved old hymn suggest?

> Dear Lord and Father of mankind,
> Forgive our foolish ways!
> Reclothe us in our rightful mind;
> In purer lives Thy service find,
> In deeper reverence, praise.
>
> ... ...
>
> Drop Thy still dews of quietness,
> Till all our strivings cease;
> Take from our souls the strain and stress,
> And let our ordered lives confess
> The beauty of Thy peace.
>
> Breathe through the heats of our desire
> Thy coolness and Thy balm;
> Let sense be dumb, let flesh retire;

> Speak through the earthquake, wind, and fire,
> O still, small voice of calm.[4]

Remain quiet, as the words of this poetic prayer describe ...

> Sitting in the silence of this waiting room with You,
> I'm ready and I'm eager for You to tell me what to do.
> I revel in Your presence, hear the whispers of Your grace,
> Shattered by the love light in Your eyes and on Your face.
>
> So hush, my soul, and listen; quit your pacing now — be still ...
> Ready all my senses to discern Your perfect will.
> Learning Your directives in the Spirit's clear air,
> Thankful in the stillness, for this priceless gift of prayer.[5]

In the frantic, frenzied rush that is my typical day, it takes time to be still in His presence. In fact, I've found that one of the secrets to loosening my tongue in order to carry on a meaningful conversation with Him is just time — time when I don't have a deadline looming. Or a clock to watch. Or the next thing on my schedule to do. It takes time to settle my mind on the Eternal and just worship Him for who He is as my prayer begins ...

I Worship You

I worship You, Jesus, Lord of Glory ...

> for leaving the throne room in heaven,
> for humbling Yourself as You took on human flesh,
> for giving Your life as a ransom for mine ...
> that my sins might be forgiven,
> that I might have a right relationship with Your Father,
> that I might come into His presence,
> that I might talk with You now.

I worship You, Jesus, Lord of Glory,

> as the Lion of Judah who reigns
>> and as the Lamb of God who redeems.
> as the Son of Man who suffered
>> and as the Son of God who saves.

I worship You for Your _____.

Fill in the blank with your own words. Don't worry. Prayer is not a performance. It's not something you do to show others how spiritual you are. Your words don't have to be eloquent, just earnest ...

Worship Him with me. Let's use the words of this majestic old hymn to lead us:

> Holy, Holy, Holy
> Lord God Almighty!
> Early in the morning our song shall rise to Thee:
> Holy, Holy, Holy! Merciful and Mighty!
> God in Three Persons, blessed Trinity!

> Holy, Holy, Holy!
> All the saints adore Thee,
> Casting down their golden crowns around the glassy sea;
> Cherubim and seraphim falling down before Thee,
> Who wert, and art, and evermore shalt be.

> Holy, Holy, Holy!
> Though the darkness hide Thee,
> Though the eye of sinful man Thy glory may not see,
> Only Thou art Holy; there is none beside Thee
> Perfect in power, in love, and purity.

Holy, Holy, Holy!

Lord God Almighty!

All Thy works shall praise Thy name in earth and sky and sea;

Holy, Holy, Holy! Merciful and Mighty!

God in Three Persons, blessed Trinity![6]

I'm Sorry

Now we need to confess our sin. I know He already knows it all. But He also knows that you and I need to say we're sorry and ask for cleansing so we are assured there are no barriers in our relationship with Him.

Living, risen Lord,

We worship You for Your holiness. You are seated on the throne at the center of the universe, high, exalted, the train of Your robe filling all that is, and you are holy, holy, holy. You have said through Isaiah that you are not some foreign God among us[7] — You are the God of Creation, the God of Abraham, Isaac, and Jacob, the God who became flesh and dwelt among us for a time, full of grace and truth.[8] We are overwhelmed — You are so great, and we are so nothing. We crown you King of our hearts and seat You on the throne of our lives. We are reduced to size ... Woe to me!

And now, would you excuse me while I pray by myself? I invite you to listen in to my confession, but I lay out these sins solely as my own:

Dear Father God,

In the light of who You are, I see myself — a hopeless, helpless, ruined sinner, no better than those whose blatant sin I criticize daily. I remember Isaiah's testimony:

"In the year that King Uzziah died, I saw the Lord *seated on a throne, high and exalted, and the train of his robe filled the temple. Above him were seraphs, each with six wings: With two wings they covered their faces, with two they covered their feet, and with two they were flying. And they were calling to one another: 'Holy, holy, holy is the* Lord *Almighty; the whole earth is full of his glory.' At the sound of their voices the doorposts and thresholds shook and the temple was filled with smoke. 'Woe to me!' I cried. 'I am ruined! For I am a man of unclean lips, and I live among a people of unclean lips, and my eyes have seen the King, the* Lord *Almighty.'"* [9]

As I reflect on Isaiah's experience, sin comes to my mind. My sin. Sin I didn't know was there, cowering in the dark recesses of my soul. Sin I've been ignoring as I sweep it under the rug of my conscious thoughts. Sin I've defended with one excuse after another. Sin that seals Your lips and deafens Your ear ... to me.[10] Worst of all, my sin — even the least sin — is so infinite in its evil and guilt that it demanded the blood of You, God incarnate, to make atonement! How could I toy with or tolerate the very thing that nailed You to the Cross?

I'm sick and tired of lying to myself, and to You, by claiming I have no sin in my life.[11] And so, dear Father, listen to Your child as I confess my sin. I have no option but to confess and don't want another option. I want to get rid of the filthy things that clog my spiritual arteries and cloud the joy on Your face. And in the penetrating light of Your holiness, I will name my sin for what it is. I won't play games anymore with the labels I give it to make it seem less like sin.[12]

Merciful God of heaven, I confess that ...

> *my prayerlessness is pride as it suggests I think I can*
> *do anything without total dependence on You . . .*
> *my exaggeration is lying as it inflates and distorts the*
> *truth to make it sound more impressive . . .*
> *my worry is unbelief as it frets over things instead*
> *of trusting You completely, even when I don't*
> *understand why . . .*
> *my gossip is stealing as it robs another person of his or*
> *her reputation . . .*

Is my prayer of confession helping you with yours? I hope so. Just make sure there is no sin between you and your Father, robbing you of the sweetness of reveling in His presence. You may want to refer back to pages 118 – 20 and refresh yourself on the list of sins described there as a means of self-examination. Like me, if you've been to the Cross and received Jesus as your Savior and Lord, you're forgiven. But sin is a constant presence in our lives, and in order to maintain a clear channel of communication with the Father, we need to confess the mistakes we've made, the sins we've committed.

So go ahead. You pray. Obviously, I won't be listening. This kind of prayer is very private. You may want to write down on a piece of paper the sins you are naming. (If you're like me you may need several sheets of paper!) Then, since you committed them one by one, when you pray, make sure you name them one by one. And remember too . . . confess your own sin, not somebody else's. I'll help you get started:

Merciful Savior, Holy Spirit, I confess that I _____

When you've finished your confession, take the paper where you've recorded your sins by the names God gives each one, then burn or tear up the paper. Now, let's meditate on these words together . . .

> There is a fountain filled with blood
> drawn from Immanuel's veins,
> And sinners plunged beneath that flood
> Lose all their guilty stains.
>
> The dying thief rejoiced to see
> That fountain in his day;
> And there may I, though vile as he,
> Wash all my sins away.[13]

To be honest, even after I confess my sin, I sometimes have trouble forgiving myself and letting go of it. It tends to haunt me with regret and remorse. I've learned by hard experience that self-flagellation can be devil-inspired. So now, when Satan comes to remind me that I am a weakling in prayer, I tell him, *Yes, I have been. But I have taken my prayerlessness and my pride to the Cross, and I know my sin is forgiven and my guilt has been atoned for.*

What sin is Satan trying to remind you of? Is it lying or adultery or abortion or jealousy or bitterness or resentment or unforgiveness or child molestation or abuse? Is it ingratitude or prayerlessness or pridefulness or casualness or hypocrisy or a critical spirit? When Satan comes to remind you of your sin, remind him that your sin has been forgiven and your guilt has been atoned for — at the Cross! It has been covered by the blood of Jesus, and you bear it no more! When Satan tries to dig up your forgiven past, settle into your quiet place of prayer and meditate on the words of yet another old hymn:

> Though Satan should buffet, though trials should come,
> Let this blest assurance control,
> That Christ has regarded my helpless estate,
> And hath shed His own blood for my soul.

It is well with my soul,
It is well with my soul,
It is well, it is well, with my soul.

My sin, oh, the bliss of this glorious thought!
My sin, not in part but the whole,
Is nailed to the cross, and I bear it no more,
Praise the Lord, praise the Lord, O my soul![14]

Thank You

Despite all the promises and reminders, sometimes the stain of my sin seems so repugnant and the gift of His grace seems so extravagant that I can hardly believe He bestows it on us ruined sinners so freely. But He does. His Word tells us, "If we confess our sins, he is faithful and just and will forgive us our sins and purify us from all unrighteousness."[15] Still, I sometimes find myself asking, *Lord, did we hear You right? Did You say* all *unrighteousness? Do You mean* all *my sin, past, present, and future? Even if it's sin I consider little and insignificant, like gossip; or medium-sized, like losing my temper; or great big, like murder and adultery and stealing? Did You really mean* all *my sin is forgiven?*

Then I hear Him whispering to my heart — listen, and you may hear Him too: "Anne, the blood of Jesus ... purifies you from all sin.... In him you have redemption through his blood, the forgiveness of sins, in accordance with the riches of God's grace.... Because it is impossible for the blood of bulls and goats to take away your sins.... Christ came into the world.... You have been made holy through the sacrifice of the body of Jesus Christ once for all.... The Holy Spirit also testifies to you about this.... Your sins and lawless acts I will remember no more."[16]

Hearing these words in my heart, I cry out in gratitude, *Thank You! Thank You! Thank You, dear Jesus, for cleansing me and washing me by Your blood! Based on Your Word, I know I am clean and forgiven. Amen.*

Whew! I feel better. Like I've had a shower after a strenuous workout! Now ... *now,* I'm finally ready to *really* talk to Him. And I sense that He is waiting, listening, gently inviting: *Therefore, Anne, since you have confidence to enter the Most Holy Place by the blood of Jesus, by a new and living way opened for you through the curtain, that is, his body, and since you have a great priest over the house of God, draw near to God with a sincere heart in full assurance of faith, having your heart sprinkled to cleanse you from a guilty conscience.*[17]

How could anyone live one more day, one more hour, one more moment ...

without having the weight of a guilty conscience removed?

without feeling clean and forgiven?

without being assured that they are right with God?

without knowing they are going to heaven?

without exchanging fear for peace?

without being known intimately and loved unconditionally?

without replacing meaningless routine with a sense of purpose?

How could anyone, anywhere live without Jesus?

Jesus, Please ...

I honestly can't imagine living my life without Jesus in the very center of my being. But there are so many who *do* live without Him. And He has called us to carry the gospel to them. So let's talk to Him about them. I have the distinct impression they are on His mind too.

Bless the Lost

Who do you know who doesn't believe in God? Or believes Jesus is a good man and maybe a great prophet but doesn't believe He is God's only Son? Or believes there are many ways to God, and Jesus is just one of them? How many people do you know who believe that when they get to heaven, if their good deeds outweigh their bad deeds, God will let them in because they deserve it?

Let's make a list of those we know who have never received Jesus by faith as their personal Savior and Lord so that we can specifically remember to pray for each one. Put today's date by each name so you'll know when you started to pray for him or her. Leave a space where you can write in the date when God answers your prayer for that person's salvation. And now let's pray for them:

Friend of sinners,

Please befriend these people [name them]: _____.
Knowing that no one can come to you "unless the Father ... draws him,"[18] we ask that You send the Holy Spirit to hover over their hearts and minds, drawing them irresistibly to You. Place in their path Jesus-lovers who transparently live lives that demand an explanation because of their ...

> *triumph over adversity*
> *peace in the midst of confusion*
> *kindness in the face of meanness*
> *love that defuses hate*
> *soft answer that turns away wrath.*

Make them so intrigued by your servants' witness that they would acknowledge and begin to seek You. Open their eyes and their ears to spiritual things, whether through a friend or a

coworker, radio or television, or magazines or books or other
printed materials. Just get their attention! Bring them to the point
of recognizing their need of You. And when they do, please, dear
Jesus, have someone, somewhere, somehow, just give them Jesus ...
and the glorious good news of the gospel! Amen.

One day while I was praying for the lost, an entire people group came
to mind[19] — people in other countries who have never even heard that
there is a God who "so loved the world that he gave his one and only Son,
that whoever believes in him shall not perish but have eternal life."[20]

And now, may I pray again with you ...?

Lord of the nations,

You are the great God of Creation who commanded, "Let light
shine out of darkness," and it did![21] Now we ask that You would
make the light of Your truth shine in the hearts of those in dark
places around the world, to give them the light of the knowledge
of Jesus Christ. Send out the Light through the Internet, through
books, through tracts, and through faithful men and women who
leave the comfort of their own countries in order to preach and
teach the gospel in foreign lands. Oh, God, judgment is coming,
and hell is filling, and we pray, please, that You would cause the
gospel to be preached "in the whole world as a testimony to all
nations," before the end comes for them personally, or before the
end of human history.[22] For the glory of Your name, amen.

I just love being here with Him, don't you? There are so many things
on my mind I want to talk to Him about — hard things and pleasant
things too. It's especially comforting to be able to bring to him in prayer
my concerns for friends and loved ones who are facing challenges and
mired in troubles ...

Bless the Hurting

There are so many hurting people around us. For me, there always seems to be one (or more!) who is hurting ... or who is sick ... or who is lost ... or who is in danger ... or who is weak ... or who is under enormous pressure or stress. Do you know someone like that? Right now I'd like to talk to Him about my friend whose sister just died unexpectedly:

Jesus, You know my friend's sister was like a mother to her. Her sister had helped raise her. Her absence must be a terrible thing, even though we all know she is with You. Please comfort my friend. Help her to be more aware of Your presence than her sister's absence.

Or maybe *you* are the one who's hurting. I'm sorry if I've been insensitive by failing to realize it may be *your* heart that's aching, *your* body that's broken. One on one, I'm not sure what to say to you. I'm afraid I might say the wrong thing. So instead, may I simply give you Jesus? He invites us to, "Come to me, all you who are weary and burdened, and I will give you rest."[23]

Would you come to Him now? He promises that, "A bruised reed he will not break, and a smoldering wick he will not snuff out."[24] He is so tender and gentle with those who are hurting, because He understands what it feels like to hurt. In fact, He announced through Isaiah:

The Spirit of the Sovereign LORD is on me, because the LORD has anointed me to preach good news to the poor. He has sent me to bind up the brokenhearted, to proclaim freedom for the captives and release from darkness for the prisoners, to proclaim the year of the LORD's favor and the day of vengeance of our God, to comfort all who mourn, and provide for those who grieve ... to bestow on them a crown of beauty instead of ashes, the oil of gladness instead of mourning, and a garment of praise instead of a spirit of despair. They will be called oaks of righteousness, a planting of the LORD for the display of his splendor.[25]

So go ahead, pour out your heart to Him: "Cast your cares on the LORD and he will sustain you."[26]

I cannot know the challenges you're facing right now, but whatever they are, take them to Jesus in prayer and trust Him to sustain you with His promises. You might offer up your burdens with words like these:

Tender Shepherd,

I bring to You my aching heart, my broken body. I cast upon You my concerns for my despondent spouse, my troubled child, my feeble parent, my stressful job, my empty wallet. Please, dear Jesus, bind up my broken heart and free me from the prison of worry. I'm doing all I can about these concerns, Lord, but it's not enough. So I'm giving them to You, trusting You to sustain me. I thank You for promising You will soothe my grief with the oil of gladness, that You will replace my spirit of despair with a garment of praise. In Your strength, not mine, may I be an oak of righteousness standing strong in the midst of this whirlwind of trouble to display the splendor of Your grace and love and strength and sufficiency. Amen.[27]

Meditate on the image of lifting up your burdens and placing them in the Shepherd's everlasting arms. Let the following words drop over you like "dews of quietness, till all your strivings cease; take from your soul the strain and stress, and let your ordered life confess the beauty of His peace."[28] Listen for the soft singing of His Spirit in your heart . . .

Be still, my soul:
the Lord is on thy side;
Bear patiently the cross of grief or pain.
Leave to thy God to order and provide;
In every change He faithful will remain.
Be still, my soul: thy best, thy heavenly Friend.
Through thorny ways leads to a joyful end.

Be still, my soul:
thy God doth undertake
To guide the future as He has the past.
Thy hope, thy confidence let nothing shake;
All now mysterious shall be bright at last.
Be still, my soul: the waves and winds still know
His voice who ruled them while He dwelt below.

Be still, my soul:
the hour is hastening on
When we shall be forever with the Lord,
When disappointment, grief, and fear are gone,
Sorrow forgot, love's purest joys restored.
Be still, my soul: when change and tears are past,
All safe and blessed we shall meet at last.[29]

Talk to your heavenly Father who loves you. And remember that one day He will take your face in His hands and wipe all your tears away ... forever![30]

Bless Our Families and Friends

Now let's talk to Him about our families. My family is never far from being uppermost in my thoughts, and today I pray,

Jesus, would You make my little granddaughters well? They've had the wretched flu. And give my daughter strength and patience as she cares for them — she has the flu too! Please keep my husband safe as he travels, and watch over my other children too. Bless my sons-in-law ... my precious Mother and Daddy ... my sisters and brothers and their families ... my husband's family ... Thank You, Lord, for keeping all these loved ones in Your care ...

This could take me awhile. I have a very large family! In fact, I have so many family members and so many friends and so many coworkers and so many organizations I'm involved with that I have had to make a list. I keep it in a little black notebook that has a tab for each day of the week. (I used to keep a card file, like a recipe box, with dividers for each day of the week, but that was too bulky to travel with.) By dividing up my family and friends into a weekly list, I don't have to weigh myself down with the burden of talking to Him about everything and everyone everyday! That would take hours.

Would you like to know how I've divided up my list? I pray for my immediate family every day, but ...

Monday I pray for members of my staff and ministry team;

Tuesday I pray for my church and the missionaries and organizations I'm involved with such as publishers, boards, and others that I support;

Wednesday I pray for the organizers of upcoming meetings where I will be speaking;

Thursday I pray for the members of my own prayer team;

Friday I pray for my extended family;

Saturday I pray for my friends; and

Sunday I go back over the week and praise God for all He has done in answer to prayer!

The way I've divided my list may not be practical for you, but think about what kind of prayer groupings would work for you. How will you divide up *your* list? Go ahead. Do it now while it's on your mind.

One thing that seems to really help me know how to talk to Jesus specifically about others is to ask the person I'm praying for how he or she *wants* me to pray. When that person does give me a specific request, I write it down in my little black notebook. If it's not possible to learn what specific prayers are desired, as I read my Bible, I just pull out a phrase or a verse and pray it for the person or organization.

Sometimes I don't even know the persons I'm praying for, but that doesn't matter. God knows them, and He knows how to find them! For example, this week on Sunday morning, I prayed the prayers of Paul *for you*:

I keep asking that the God of our Lord Jesus Christ, the glorious Father, may give you the Spirit of wisdom and revelation, so that you may know him better. I pray also that the eyes of your heart may be enlightened in order that you may know the hope to which he has called you, the riches of his glorious inheritance in the saints, and his incomparably great power for us who believe. . . .

I pray that out of his glorious riches he may strengthen you with power through his Spirit in your inner being, so that Christ may dwell in your heart through faith. And I pray that you, being rooted and established in love, may have power, together with all the saints, to grasp how wide and long and high and deep is the love of Christ, and to know this love that surpasses knowledge — that you may be filled to the measure of all the fullness of God . . .

For this reason, since the day I heard about you [and prayed that this book would fall into your hands], I have not stopped

*praying for you and asking God to fill you with the knowledge of
his will through all spiritual wisdom and understanding. And I
pray this in order that you may live a life worthy of the Lord and
may please him in every way: bearing fruit in every good work,
growing in the knowledge of God, being strengthened with all
power according to his glorious might so that you may have great
endurance and patience, and joyfully giving thanks to the Father,
who has qualified you to share in the inheritance of the saints in
the kingdom of light.[31] For Jesus' sake, Amen.*

Sorry for being a little long-winded, but thank you for letting me
pray for you. And would you please pray for me also? I would be hon-
ored if you would put me somewhere on your weekly prayer list.[32]

Bless the Church

As we pray for friends and family, I can't help but think of our larger
family — the family of God we call the church. Many of our Christian
brothers and sisters in the church worldwide are suffering for the sake
of Jesus and paying the ultimate price for their faith in Him.

My prayers for these brave Christians are inspired by the extraordinary words of the first-century Christians as they faced violent persecution. They didn't pray for deliverance; they prayed for the Lord to
"consider their threats and enable your servants to speak your word
with great boldness."[33] And that's my prayer for the persecuted church
around the world, while at the same time I also climb inside our Lord's
own prayer to His Father and implore Him to deliver them from evil.[34]

The church around the world seems to do so much for Jesus, even
though they seem to have so little in the way of resources and education. The church in the Western World, on the other hand, seems to do
relatively little for Jesus while we have so much in the way of resources
and education. Sometimes I think our churches are a mile wide in

knowledge but an inch deep in real understanding and discipleship. We have been blessed in so many ways, yet we desperately need a fresh touch from God.

I have borrowed the words of Daniel, the prophet, as he prayed for Jerusalem, as words to use in my own prayer for our churches:

Now, our God, hear the prayers and petitions of your servant. For your sake, O Lord, look with favor on your desolate sanctuary. Give ear, O God, and hear; open your eyes and see the desolation of the [church] that bears your Name. We do not make requests of you because we are righteous, but because of your great mercy. O Lord, listen! O Lord, forgive! O Lord, hear and act! For your sake, O my God, do not delay, because your [church] and your people bear your Name.[35]

What church do you go to? How many people are led to faith in Jesus Christ each week? Each month? Each year? *Anyone?* Are marriages reconciled and relationships healed? *No?* Is God's Word preached with power from the pulpit? *Ever?* Is the gospel central to every activity and program? (That's not the same as an elective class offered on how to present the four spiritual laws.) How many people attend prayer meeting? What's that? *You don't even have* a regularly scheduled prayer meeting in your church?

I think we need to talk to Jesus together about our churches.

Jesus, help us! Send out a wake-up call and then pour out Your Spirit upon Your people once again. Bring each of us back to the foot of the Cross. Convict us of our sin that we might repent and be cleansed by Your blood. Give us churches whose pulpits and pews are filled with Isaiahs, fire-filled Christians whose knowledge of You has dropped the eighteen inches from their heads to their hearts.

We ask that You raise up godly pastors to preach to us and godly men and women to lead us and godly congregations that love You and love each other. Call forth a church that doesn't just have a form of godliness but possesses real power to change lives,[36] demonstrating to the watching world what society in general would be like if it were under Your authority. Give believers a hunger for Your Word that they might be stalwarts for the truth, living humbly, boldly, and righteously for You. We hold You to Your promise, that "if my people, who are called by my name, will humble themselves and pray and seek my face and turn from their wicked ways, then will I hear from heaven and will forgive their sin and will heal their land."[37]

Did that last phrase catch your attention, too? That God will heal and bless our nation when you and I get right with Him? Many of us in the United States pray, *God bless America*. But isn't it interesting that His blessing is directly related, not to politics or to public policy or to government programs or to social justice or to racial equality or to welfare reform or taxation or education or health care or affordable housing — but it's directly related to *the church getting right with Him*?

What can we do about the dismal, declining moral and spiritual condition of the church today? We can talk to Him about it. We can pray for revival in our day as Isaiah prayed for revival in his: *"O God, that you would rend the heavens and come down" once again!*[38]

Historic revival has almost always begun with a longing in one person's heart that became a prayer burden and then led to broader, corporate prayer. The First Great Awakening in our own nation (1734 – 1750) was triggered when Jonathan Edwards read an article on revival then began to pray, urging churches everywhere to pray in a synchronized effort he called "concerts of prayer."

Following the moral decline after the American Revolution, a single pastor, Isaac Backus, began to pray. He then pleaded with pastors all over the country, calling them to pray on the first Monday every month for revival. They did — and the Second Great Awakening (1790 – 1840) erupted.

In South Africa, thirty years of prayer preceded the outpouring of God's Spirit at Worcester in 1860.

In 1904, a simple Welsh coal miner began to agonize in prayer over the state of the church. As he prayed and then shared his burden, the wind of the Spirit blew over the few sparks of life, and the fire of revival broke out in Wales.

In 1949, the great revival of Hebrides began with the longing of one church and the prayers of two older, blind, arthritic women.

As a result of these revivals, Christians have returned to a holy lifestyle, millions of people have been saved, and God has exalted a passionate love for Jesus Christ in the hearts of His people. The founding of orphanages, hospitals, and halfway houses as well as the achievement of racial equality, social justice, and even a clean environment all have roots in the revival of the church.

While historic, corporate revival has been different each time God has chosen to send it, some elements have been consistently the same. One of those elements is prayer. If God used the prayer of one person in the past to spark revival in that person's day, why couldn't He do it again? What could be holding Him back in our day? Is it possible that no one is truly burdened, no one is really desperate, and no one is earnestly praying for revival? I'm not sure we will ever know what God would do in answer to one person's prayer, unless we are willing to be that one person. And so I have asked myself, *Anne, if revival in your family, in your church, in your city, in your state, in your nation, depended upon your prayer life, would it ever come?* I wonder . . .

I think I'd better talk to Him about it . . .

The Second Log for the Revival Fire: Listen to Him

Hasn't our prayer time together been wonderful? I don't want it to end. I can already feel the revival fire burning in my heart. But I think it's time we added the second log to the fire. The second log is Bible reading.

My friend Thomas, whom I mentioned previously, related that when he was a young boy, a very well-meaning neighborhood woman had forced him, along with her son and other playmates, to read the Bible and memorize Scripture. He described how he hated it at the time because his active little body much preferred running and jumping and playing and throwing a ball and biking and hiking. The forced Bible-reading sessions produced a strong aversion to the Scriptures that carried over into his adulthood.[39]

Following his experience of personal revival, he described going back, in his mind's eye, to the living room of the neighborhood woman. But this time Jesus was there, beckoning Thomas to join him in the big, overstuffed chair by the bay window. As Jesus held out His arms, Thomas imagined himself climbing up into His lap. Then Jesus opened up the Bible and began to read to him.

With eyes filled with the thrill of discovery, Thomas looked at me and exclaimed, "Anne, the Bible is His Word! It's living! I love it! Now I can't read it enough!"

Like Thomas, have you had an aversion to reading the Bible? Have you thought it was boring or irrelevant or confusing? Then I want to invite you to climb up into the Lord's lap and let Him "read" it to you. Hearing His voice within its pages will transform your aversion into a lifetime of joyful discovery and keep you seeing Him ... *always.*

Let me share with you how you can read His Word in a way that lets you hear His voice speaking to you personally through its pages. In the Appendix you will find five Scripture-study worksheets designed to help you get started in listening to God's voice as you read your Bible. Ideally you will complete one a day, so you'll finish them all in less than a week. The worksheets lead you through my own system of very meaningful meditation. They are simple and easy, practical and personal. Follow the instructions, and you will see how this exercise teaches you to listen to God's voice.

For some, hearing Him speak is like a quiet knowing. For others, it's more electric — as though the verses had bells, whistles, and flashing neon lights. Regardless of how His voice "sounds" to you, the impact will be like fuel that keeps the fire burning in your heart.

So ... make sure, before closing this book, that you add the logs of daily prayer and Bible reading to your fire.

You Are the Firekeeper

Don't let the revival fire die down! If you have read this book and do nothing, regardless of how meaningful it has been, the fire that has been kindled in your heart will flicker, die down, and go out. You are the keeper of the fire.

In the olden days of the Roman Empire, there was, of course, no electricity. You could not flip a switch to turn on a light or twist a knob to heat your stove or push a button on your thermostat to increase the warmth of your home. Instead, every village had a fire that burned in the central plaza twenty-four hours a day, seven days a week. The fire was considered so vital to the life of the village that a firekeeper was hired to keep it burning. If for any reason the fire went out — whether neglect allowed it to slowly die or a windstorm blew it out or a rainstorm drenched it — it cost the firekeeper his life.

God has given you and me the fire of the Spirit with all of His passionate energy and love for Jesus. If you let the fire go out — for any reason — it will cost you your life. Not your eternal salvation but the vitality of your spiritual life, the fullness of God's blessing, the abundant life Jesus came to give you. Don't quench the fire of the Spirit by your neglect of daily Bible reading and prayer. Don't grieve Him by your sin. Fan the flame! *You're the firekeeper of your heart!*

So . . .

> Stir up the fire!
> Throw on the logs!
> Talk to Him!
> Listen to Him!
> Fan into flame your love for Jesus!
> STAY AWAKE!

. . . until your faith becomes sight and you can exclaim, "I saw the Lord!"

Epilogue

Toward the end of Isaiah's life, his awestruck worship and wonder could still be heard as he relived the fresh encounter he had had with God back in the year that King Uzziah died. The experience that was emblazoned forever in his memory must have leaped to life as his pen flowed across the page, writing, "For this is what the high and lofty One says — he who lives forever, whose name is holy: 'I live in a high and holy place, but also with him who is contrite and lowly in spirit, to revive the spirit of the lowly and to revive the heart of the contrite.'"[1]

Isaiah's personal revival lasted a lifetime because it was the direct result of his ongoing, intimate relationship with the Lord.

While Isaiah achieved greatness in God's eyes, his beloved nation of Judah did not. As a result of its wickedness and rebellion, God's people came under God's judgment and were carried off into captivity by the Babylonians.

Traditional history tells us that before God's judgment fell, wicked King Manasseh had Isaiah stuffed into a hollow tree trunk then sawn in two. God notes his martyrdom in the vividly descriptive "Hall of Faith" recorded in Hebrews 11:

> And what more shall I say? I do not have time to tell about Gideon, Barak, Samson, Jephthah, David, Samuel and the prophets, who through faith conquered kingdoms, administered justice, and gained what was promised; who shut the mouths of lions, quenched

the fury of the flames, and escaped the edge of the sword; whose weakness was turned to strength; and who became powerful in battle and routed foreign armies. Women received back their dead, raised to life again. Others were tortured and refused to be released, so that they might gain a better resurrection. Some faced jeers and flogging, while still others were chained and put in prison. They were stoned; *they were sawn in two*; they were put to death by the sword. They went about in sheepskins and goatskins, destitute, persecuted and mistreated — the world was not worthy of them. They wandered in deserts and mountains, and in caves and holes in the ground.

These were all commended for their faith, yet none of them received what had been promised [the Messiah who is Jesus]. God had planned something better for us [the fulfillment of all the promises in Christ, the Cross, and our redemption] so that only together with us would they be made perfect.[2]

More Than a Wake-up Call ...

My sincere prayer is that this book has been a wake-up call for your heart. But I pray it's been more than that ...

I pray that the eyes of your heart have been opened, giving you a fresh vision of the Lord, "seated on his throne, high and exalted" (Isaiah 6:1).

I pray that as you've read these words your knowledge has dropped the eighteen inches from your head to your heart.

I pray that you've felt the fire of personal revival ignited within you.

I pray that the revival you've experienced will last forever.

I pray that your life will be contagious and the fire will spread.

I pray that, as a result of the fire in your heart, the whole church
   will be revived and rekindled with fire from above until she
   is holy, cleansed, and one day presentable to the Lord of Glory
   as a radiant Bride![3]

࠵

Let us rejoice and be glad

and give him glory!

For the wedding of the Lamb has come,

and his bride has made herself ready.

<small>REVELATION 19:7</small>

Scripture-Study Worksheets to Help You Keep the Revival Fire Burning

Over the years, I've developed a way to read God's Word so that I more clearly hear His voice speaking to me personally through the pages of the Bible. The five Scripture-study worksheets here are designed to help you get started in listening to God's voice as you read your Bible. Ideally you will complete one a day, so you'll finish them all in less than a week. The worksheets lead you through my personal system of very meaningful meditation. I hope you find my method as revealing and insightful as it has been for me. Please set aside some quiet time in the next five days to begin this important first step in keeping the revival fire burning within you.*

Each step below corresponds to a section on the worksheets. As you read through the instructions for each step, you may wish to refer to the completed example for Mark 9:2–8 on pages 207–10.

*Feel free to write in the blank spaces if you own the book. If you've borrowed it from a library, however, please write your answers on a separate sheet of paper so that others may use this book as well.

SCRIPTURE-STUDY
WORKSHEET INSTRUCTIONS

STEP ONE *Read God's Word.*

Begin by reading a brief passage of Scripture (one paragraph or so). The Scripture-study exercises included here focus on short passages of two to eight verses each.

Don't rush. Read God's Word prayerfully, objectively, thoughtfully, attentively. The object of this devotional exercise is not to get through a passage, or even to study a passage, but to maintain the fire of revival in your heart as you hear from Him.

STEP TWO *What does God's Word say?*
List the facts.

Make a verse-by-verse list of the outstanding facts as you see them in the passage. Pinpoint the most obvious facts. Do not paraphrase or put His words into your own but use the actual words from the passage itself. Leave out secondary details and start with the nouns and verbs.

STEP THREE *What does God's Word mean?*
Learn the lessons.

Go back to the list of facts and look for a lesson or spiritual principle to learn in each fact. Ask yourself, "What are the people in this passage doing or not doing that I should be doing or not doing? Is there a command I should obey? A promise I should claim? A warning I should heed? An example I should follow?"

STEP FOUR *What does God's Word mean to me?*
Listen to His voice.

Take the lessons or principles from step three and put them in the form of a question you could ask yourself, your spouse, your child, a friend, a neighbor, or a coworker. As you do so, listen for God to speak to you personally through His Word. This is the most meaningful step, the one in which I so frequently hear God's voice. But you cannot do step four until steps one, two, and three are completed. No skipping steps!

If you're someone who has trouble settling down and waiting quietly to hear the still, small voice of God, don't be discouraged if it takes awhile to develop this ability to focus single-mindedly so that everything else around you seems to temporarily fade away. The more time you spend in this prayerful, meditative, listening mode, the clearer God's voice will become. And please don't be put off by the completed examples, thinking, *I would* never *have thought of that!* The meanings will come to you as you meditate and open your mind to God's Spirit.

STEP FIVE *How will I respond to God's Word today?*
Live it out.

Listen for God to speak to you personally through the passage. He may not speak to you through every verse, but He *will* speak. When He does, record the verse number, what it is He seems to be saying to you, and your response to Him. You may wish to also note the date, both as a means of keeping a journal and to hold yourself accountable to an obedient response.

When you complete the five Scripture-study worksheets, use the same method to study your favorite Bible passages.

Remember, your aim is not to get through the passage but to listen to God's voice in the passage. So apply the format to just one paragraph of Scripture at a time. If you desire further help or materials, please contact me at:

> AnGeL Ministries
> 5115 Hollyridge Drive
> Raleigh, NC 27612 – 3111
> 919 787-6606

You may also email me at *info@angelministries.org* or contact me through our website: *www.AnneGrahamLotz.com.*

COMPLETED EXAMPLE OF A
SCRIPTURE-STUDY WORKSHEET

Mark 9:2–8

STEP ONE

Read God's Word.

v.2. After six days Jesus took Peter, James and John with him and led them up a high mountain, where they were all alone. There he was transfigured before them.

v.3. His clothes became dazzling white, whiter than anyone in the world could bleach them.

v.4. And there appeared before them Elijah and Moses, who were talking with Jesus.

v.5. Peter said to Jesus, "Rabbi, it is good for us to be here. Let us put up three shelters — one for you, one for Moses and one for Elijah."

v.6. (He did not know what to say, they were so frightened.)

v.7. Then a cloud appeared and enveloped them, and a voice came from the cloud: "This is my Son, whom I love. Listen to him!"

v.8. Suddenly, when they looked around, they no longer saw anyone with them except Jesus.

STEP TWO

What does God's Word say? List the facts.

v.2. Jesus took Peter, James, and John alone up a mountain, where He was transfigured before them.

v.3. His clothes became dazzling white.

v.4. Moses and Elijah appeared before them, talking with Jesus.

v.5. Peter said, "It is good to be here. Let us put up three shelters."

v.6. He didn't know what to say.

v.7. A voice came from the cloud saying, "This is my Son. Listen to Him."

v.8. Suddenly they no longer saw anyone except Jesus.

STEP THREE

What does God's Word mean? Learn the lessons.

v.2. Jesus wants to spend time alone with us.

v.3. When we make the time to be alone with Jesus, He has the opportunity to give us a fresh vision of Himself.

v.4. The entire Bible, Old and New Testaments, is focused on Jesus.

v.5. While we love mountaintop experiences, sometimes we think of Jesus as just another man equal in honor to the prophets.

v.6. Sometimes our emotions prompt us to speak when we should be silent.

v.7. We are commanded by God to listen to what Jesus says.

v.8. When everything else fades away, including our visions and experiences of revival and glory, our focus should still be on Jesus.

STEP FOUR

What does God's Word mean to me? Listen to His voice.

v.2. When have I spent time alone with Jesus? Will I use the following worksheets as my way of accepting His invitation to spend time with Him, crawl up into His lap, and listen to His voice?

v.3. What fresh vision of Jesus will I receive as I spend time alone with Him in His Word each day?

v.4. As I read my Bible, where is my focus?

v.5. When have I wanted to linger in the feelings of an experience while downplaying who Jesus is?

v.6. When have my words and works interrupted my worship?

v.7. Am I willing now to obey God's command and *listen* to the voice of His beloved Son?

v.8. Following an emotional experience or the spiritual high of revival, what will I do to fan the flames, keep the revival fire going, and make sure I see Jesus only ... always?

STEP FIVE

How will I respond to God's Word today? Live it out.

I long to see Jesus always. I don't want the fire of revival to burn out in my heart. I want to hear from Jesus. So I choose to make time each day, beginning today, to get away and be alone with and read His Word, listening for His voice to speak to me personally as I keep my focus on Him.

NOW IT'S YOUR TURN: SCRIPTURE-STUDY WORKSHEET ONE

Revelation 1:1–3

Now that I've shown you how it's done, here are worksheets focusing on five more passages of Scripture. Read the passages slowly, then thoughtfully fill in the blanks. This first worksheet includes examples that take you through steps two through five as you study verse 1. Use these examples to get started, but please don't let them hinder you from finding your own answers for verse 1 as well as for the other verses.

STEP ONE

Read God's Word.

v.1.　The revelation of Jesus Christ, which God gave him to show his servants what must soon take place. He made it known by sending his angel to his servant John,

v.2.　who testifies to everything he saw — that is, the word of God and the testimony of Jesus Christ.

v.3.　Blessed is the one who reads the words of this prophecy, and blessed are those who hear it and take to heart what is written in it, because the time is near.

STEP TWO

What does God's Word say? List the facts.

Example:

v.1.　God gave the revelation of Jesus Christ, making it known to John to show His servants what must take place.

STEP THREE

What does God's Word mean? Learn the lessons.

Example:

v.1. God reveals Jesus to His servants through His Word.

STEP FOUR

What does God's Word mean to me? Listen to His voice.

Example:

v.1. As I long to see Jesus always, where am I looking?

STEP FIVE

How will I respond to God's Word today? Live it out.

Example:

As I read my Bible each day, I choose to open my eyes to see Jesus ... and to open my ears to hear His voice.

SCRIPTURE-STUDY WORKSHEET TWO

Revelation 1:4–8

STEP ONE

STEP TWO

Read God's Word.

What does God's Word say? List the facts.

v.4. John, To the seven churches
in the province of Asia: Grace
and peace to you from him
who is, and who was, and who
is to come, and from the seven
spirits before his throne,

v.5. and from Jesus Christ, who
is the faithful witness, the
firstborn from the dead, and
the ruler of the kings of the
earth. To him who loves us and
has freed us from our sins by
his blood,

v.6. and has made us to be a
kingdom and priests to serve
his God and Father — to him
be glory and power for ever
and ever! Amen.

v.7. Look, he is coming with the
clouds, and every eye will see
him, even those who pierced
him; and all the peoples of the
earth will mourn because of
him. So shall it be! Amen.

v.8. "I am the Alpha and the
Omega," says the Lord God,
"who is, and who was, and who
is to come, the Almighty."

STEP THREE

What does God's Word mean? Learn the lessons.

STEP FOUR

What does God's Word mean to me? Listen to His voice.

STEP FIVE

How will I respond to God's Word today? Live it out.

SCRIPTURE-STUDY WORKSHEET THREE

Revelation 1:9–11

STEP ONE

STEP TWO

Read God's Word

What does God's Word say? List the facts.

v.9.   I, John, your brother and
        companion in the suffering
        and kingdom and patient
        endurance that are ours in
        Jesus, was on the island of
        Patmos because of the word
        of God and the testimony of
        Jesus.

v.10. On the Lord's Day I was in the
        Spirit, and I heard behind me a
        loud voice like a trumpet,

v.11. which said: "Write on a scroll
        what you see and send it to the
        seven churches: to Ephesus,
        Smyrna, Pergamum, Thyatira,
        Sardis, Philadelphia and
        Laodicea."

STEP THREE

What does God's Word mean? Learn the lessons.

STEP FOUR

What does God's Word mean to me? Listen to His voice.

STEP FIVE

How will I respond to God's Word today? Live it out.

SCRIPTURE-STUDY WORKSHEET FOUR

Revelation 1:12 – 16

STEP ONE	STEP TWO

Read God's Word.

v.12. I turned around to see the voice that was speaking to me. And when I turned I saw seven golden lampstands,

v.13. and among the lampstands was someone "like a son of man," dressed in a robe reaching down to his feet and with a golden sash round his chest.

v.14. His head and hair were white like wool, as white as snow, and his eyes were like blazing fire.

v.15. His feet were like bronze glowing in a furnace, and his voice was like the sound of rushing waters.

v.16. In his right hand he held seven stars, and out of his mouth came a sharp double-edged sword. His face was like the sun shining in all its brilliance.

What does God's Word say? List the facts.

STEP THREE

What does God's Word mean? Learn the lessons.

STEP FOUR

What does God's Word mean to me? Listen to His voice.

STEP FIVE

How will I respond to God's Word today? Live it out.

SCRIPTURE-STUDY WORKSHEET FIVE

Revelation 1:17–20

STEP ONE	**STEP TWO**

Read God's Word.

v.17. When I saw him, I fell at his feet as though dead. Then he placed his right hand on me and said: "Do not be afraid. I am the First and the Last.

v.18. I am the Living One; I was dead, and behold I am alive for ever and ever! And I hold the keys of death and Hades.

v.19. Write, therefore, what you have seen, what is now and what will take place later.

v.20. The mystery of the seven stars that you saw in my right hand and of the seven golden lampstands is this: The seven stars are the angels of the seven churches, and the seven lampstands are the seven churches."

What does God's Word say? List the facts.

STEP THREE

STEP FOUR

What does God's Word mean? Learn the lessons.

What does God's Word mean to me? Listen to His voice.

STEP FIVE

How will I respond to God's Word today? Live it out.

Notes

A Wake-up Call
(pages 13 – 23)

1. See Luke 12:16 – 21.

A Longing to See Jesus ... Again
(pages 25 – 29)

1. God did open a window of time that allowed me an extended visit with my parents. I soaked up every precious, priceless minute. While I was home, Daddy had to leave for a meeting, and I was left looking forward to heaven, where there will be no more separation from those we love!

2. The definitions of revival were given by the following men in corresponding order to the way they appear on page 27: Robert Coleman; Erwin Lutzer; Duncan Campbell; D.M. Patton; Vance Havner; from Dale Schlafer, *Revival 101* (Colorado Springs: Navpress, 2003), 11.

3. *Newsweek*, September 5, 2005, 48, 50.

ONE ～ You're Sleeping!
(pages 31 – 56)

1. On September 14, 2005, Lawrence Karlton, a federal district judge in San Francisco, ruled that the Pledge of Allegiance is unconstitutional because the phrase "under God" violates public school students' right to be "free from a coercive requirement to affirm God," as reported by CNN.com.

2. Judah was a land that had once been part of the kingdom of Israel. God initially promised Abraham that if he followed Him in a life of faith, He would establish Abraham's family as a nation through which the entire world would be blessed. (See Genesis 12:1 – 3.) Four generations later, God kept His promise, and the nation was established with Abraham's twelve great-grandsons forming the twelve tribes of Israel. The nation subsequently became the kingdom of Israel. The 120 years of its existence were equally divided by the reigns of three kings: Saul, David, and Solomon.

Following Solomon's death, the kingdom of Israel was divided. Ten tribes formed the northern kingdom, which was called Israel, while the two remaining tribes became the southern kingdom known as Judah.

The northern kingdom was in existence two hundred years before being destroyed by Assyria in 722 BC. The southern kingdom lasted three hundred years, until it was destroyed by Babylon around 586 BC. God raised up Isaiah in 741 BC as His spokesman to both kingdoms during the time that preceded His judgment on them.

3. See Isaiah 26:19; Romans 13:11; Ephesians 5:14; and Revelation 3:3.

4. See 2 Kings 21:1 – 16.

5. See Isaiah 3:14 – 15.

6. See Isaiah 3:15.

7. See Isaiah 1:23.

8. See Isaiah 1:23.

9. See Isaiah 1:12 – 14.

10. See 2 Timothy 3:1, 5.

11. See Matthew 7:21 – 23.

12. See Romans 12:2; 2 Corinthians 6:17.

13. 2 Chronicles 7:13 – 14.

14. Ibid.

15. Revelation 2:18.

16. While 9/11 was a wake-up call to America, it was also a wicked deed perpetrated on innocent people. The attackers would do well to consider that although God used Assyria and Babylon as his instruments of

judgment against Israel and Judah, eventually they too were destroyed by God for their wickedness and evil.

17. Psalm 119:89.

18. Matthew 5:18.

19. See Galatians 3:24 KJV.

20. Isaiah 1:2, emphasis mine.

21. Isaiah 1:10, emphasis mine.

22. Isaiah 1:10, emphasis mine.

23. Isaiah 1:11, emphasis mine.

24. Isaiah 1:18, emphasis mine.

25. Isaiah 1:20, emphasis mine.

26. Isaiah 1:24, emphasis mine.

27. John 14:6.

28. Ibid.

29. Genesis 1:1.

30. Isaiah 64:6.

31. Romans 3:10.

32. Acts 4:12.

33. John 3:16.

34. Like Isaiah, the church today has the Word of God and knows its truth. But knowing what is true and having the impetus to preach it boldly in word and deed are two different things. It was Isaiah's personal revival, his vision of the Lord, that took the message from his head to his heart — and then from his heart to the people who so desperately needed to hear it.

TWO ~ Wake Up!
(pages 57 – 71)

1. Ezekiel 1:4 – 5.

2. At the time of Uzziah's death, he himself was not living in the king's

palace but in a separate house (see 2 Chronicles 26:21).

3. *People* magazine, January 17, 2005, 97.

4. Psalm 6:6.

5. King Uzziah "did what was right in the eyes of the LORD. . . . His fame spread far and wide, for he was greatly helped until he became powerful. But after Uzziah became powerful, his pride led to his downfall. He was unfaithful to the LORD his God" (2 Chronicles 26:4, 15, 16). Uzziah actually ended his life as a leper, living in a separate house from the palace, and was excluded from the temple (see 2 Chronicles 26:21).

6. I've put this story together using information from the websites *www.first-to-fly.com* and *www.centennialofflight.gov*, and also from the Dayton (Ohio) Metro Library, which offers online viewing of some of the items in its Wright Brothers Collection, including newspaper clippings and other items preserved in the Wright brothers' own scrapbooks: *http://webster.daytonmetrolibrary.org/localhistory.cfm.*

7. John 12:41.

8. According to the Bible, Jesus Christ is the eternal God who became a human person when He was born as a baby in Bethlehem (see John 1:1 – 2, 14 and Philippians 2:5 – 6). His birth and subsequent life on earth are referred to as the "incarnation" of God, which simply means God became human without in any way being diminished in His deity. Jesus Christ is not half God and half man. He is fully God and fully man. To refer to Him as "pre-incarnate" is to refer to Him before He took on humanity.

THREE ~ Open Your Eyes!
(pages 73 – 101)

1. 1 John 1:5.

2. The Palace of Shushan has been excavated, and archeologists believe it was actually one of the residences of King Artaxerxes of Persia and his empress, Queen Esther.

3. The tabernacle was a portable sanctuary that contained all that was necessary for worship as the children of Israel wandered in the wilderness. It also served as something of a prototype for a permanent structure that was built during the reign of King Solomon. The Tabernacle typified God's dwelling among His people. (Adapted from J. D. Douglas, *The New International Dictionary of the Bible* [Grand Rapids, MI: Zondervan, 1999.])

4. See Exodus 26:7, 14.

5. The word *Shekinah* in Hebrew literally means "the dwelling of God." Although not a biblical term, it is used to describe the visible presence of the Lord. (See Douglas, *The New International Dictionary of the Bible.*)

6. This same principle becomes very personal when we read Paul's lesson to the Corinthians that "we have this treasure [the glory of God] in jars of clay [our own bodies and lives] to show that this all-surpassing power is from God and not from us" (2 Corinthians 4:7). Looking at you and me, who would ever suspect that wrapped within us is the very glory and character and nature of God?

7. Emphasis mine.

8. See John 12:41.

9. See Psalm 89:8.

10. See Isaiah 64:4 and 1 Corinthians 2:9 – 10.

11. See John 1:40.

12. See Proverbs 3:5 – 6.

13. See Romans 8:28.

14. Revelation 4:1, 2.

15. John 20:14.

16. See Romans 8:34.

17. See 1 Peter 1:3.

18. See John 14:2 – 3.

19. See 2 Corinthians 1:20.

20. See John 3:16.

21. See Luke 5:24.

22. See John 1:12.

23. See John 17:2.

24. See John 14:16 – 17.

25. See Luke 10:19.

26. See Ephesians 1:11 – 12.

27. See John 14:2 – 3.

28. See John 1:1; Colossians 1:15 – 17; 2 Corinthians 4:6.

29. See Amos 4:13; 5:8.

30. See Luke 8:24 – 25.

31. See Matthew 8:28 – 32.

32. See Mark 11:23.

33. See Matthew 9:2 – 7; 11:5.

34. See Mark 7:32 – 35.

35. See Mark 10:46 – 52 and John 9:1 – 7.

36. See Luke 17:11 – 19.

37. See Mark 5:35 – 42 and John 11:38 – 44.

38. See John 14:1 – 6 and Revelation 22:12 – 14.

39. See Isaiah 2:6 – 8.

40. See Joshua 24:31; Romans 9:4 – 5; John 1:16.

41. See Exodus 7 – 12.

42. See Exodus 14:21 – 22.

43. See Exodus 14:23 – 28.

44. See Exodus 16.

45. See Exodus 17:1 – 7.

46. See Exodus 20:1 – 17; Exodus 21 – 40; and the book of Leviticus.

47. See Joshua 3:14 – 17.

48. See Joshua 6:1 – 20.

49. See Joshua 23:9 – 10.

50. See Numbers 13:27; Deuteronomy 6:10 – 12; and Joshua 24:2 – 13.

51. See Hebrews 11:32 – 38.

52. See John 1:1 – 2.

53. See Deuteronomy 7:7 – 9.

54. See John 1:11 – 14, 17 – 18.

55. Hebrews 13:5.

56. See Psalm 139:7 – 12.

57. Ezekiel 48:35, emphasis mine.

58. See 1 Corinthians 3:16.

59. See 1 John 1:7 – 9.

60. See John 3:15 – 16.

61. See Revelation 3:20; Luke 11:13; Ephesians 1:13.

62. See John 1:12.

63. Ephesians 5:18.

64. See Acts 4:31.

65. See Acts 17:6.

66. Revelation 5:12.

67. Revelation 5:13.

68. Philippians 2:9 – 11.

69. See Acts 2:4, 14 – 36, 41.

70. See Psalm 22:3 KJV.

71. See Isaiah 61:3.

72. See Psalm 18:3.

73. See Psalm 43:5.

74. See Exodus 13:21.

75. See Exodus 34:29 – 35.

76. See Exodus 40:34 – 35.

77. See Ezekiel 10:18 and Psalm 137:1 – 2.

78. Revelation 4:8; 5:11 – 12.

79. Compare Revelation 4:4 with Isaiah 6:3.

80. See 1 Peter 1:16.

81. See Revelation 2:18 – 29.

FOUR ∾ Rend Your Heart!
(pages 103 – 21)

1. See John 20:15.

2. Joel 2:13.

3. Luke 5:5.

4. Luke 5:8.

5. This statement is a poor paraphrase of a comment I remember from John Trapp, an old-world theologian who is one of my mother's favorite authors.

6. Joel 2:13.

7. Romans 7:18.

8. See Ezekiel 1:28; Acts 9:4; and Revelation 1:17.

9. See Isaiah 57:15.

10. Matthew 7:3 – 5.

11. See Mark 12:30 – 31.

12. When I was a young girl, I was convicted of my sinful state while watching on TV a movie entitled *King of Kings* (directed by Cecil B. DeMille), a portrayal of the life of Christ. In prayer, I told God I was a sinner, I believed Jesus had died on the Cross as His sacrifice for my sin, and I asked Him to forgive me and come into my heart. I believe by faith that He heard my little-girl prayer, forgave me of my sin, and placed His Spirit within me. I believe I was born again into His family at that time. I know I am forgiven and that when I die I will go to heaven. But I am still a sinner.

13. See Romans 8:1 – 4.

14. I am grateful to a nineteenth-century revivalist, Charles G. Finney, for help with this list, which I have used to examine my own life. I found it in his book *How to Experience Revival* (New Kensington, PA: Whitaker House, 1984), 18 – 27.

15. See James 4:17.

FIVE ~ Bend Your Knees!
(pages 123 – 36)

1. The blood of Jesus shed on the Cross is obviously represented by the coal of fire since the Cross is the only place anyone can have guilt removed and sin atoned for.

2. My personalized paraphrase of 1 John 1:7. When I place my faith in Jesus Christ as my Savior, all my sin is forgiven. Even future sin is forgiven because all the sin of my entire life was future when He died on the Cross to forgive me. "The blood of Jesus ... purifies us from every sin" (1 John 1:7).

3. My paraphrase of 1 John 1:9.

4. Isaiah 1:18.

5. My paraphrase of Psalm 103:12.

6. See Romans 8:33 – 34.

7. See Micah 7:19.

8. You may want to work through the section titled "The First Log of the Revival Fire: Talk to Him" in chapter 8 for further help in bringing your sin to the Cross right now.

9. Galatians 2:20.

10. Revelation 1:17.

11. Revelation 1:17, 19, emphasis mine.

12. See Mark 3:17; Luke 9:51 – 55.

13. The calling of John to be a disciple gives wonderful hope and encouragement to all of us who are ordinary men and women with human failings and frailties! See

1 Corinthians 1:26 – 31 for further encouragement.

14. For example, see Acts 3:1 – 8.

15. The biography of Jesus, which is the fourth to be found in the New Testament, is entitled simply the Gospel of John.

16. Read 1 John and count the number of times the apostle John addresses the reader as "dear children," or "dear friends."

17. John's eyewitness account of the end of human history is the last book of the Bible, the Revelation of Jesus Christ.

18. See Revelation 1:9.

19. John 3:16.

20. See Romans 8:30.

21. Thomas's name has been changed to protect his identity, but the conversation described is authentic.

22. See Isaiah 7:3; 8:1, 3, 5, 11 (emphasis mine).

SIX ~ Just Say Yes!
(pages 137 – 49)

1. John 10:3, 4.

2. Anne Graham Lotz, *Daily Light* (Nashville: J. Countryman, 1998), February 3. I have inserted my name into the verses and changed the pronouns in order to help you "hear" the way the Shepherd spoke to me that morning.

3. John 4:35 and Luke 10:2 – 3.

4. Matthew 28:19 – 20.

5. Exodus 4:13.

SEVEN ∾ Move Your Feet!

(pages 151–63)

1. Ezekiel 1:28; 2:3.

2. Acts 26:14–17.

3. Acts 26:19.

4. Revelation 1:17, 19.

5. See John 21:10–18.

6. 2 Corinthians 5:14–15.

7. 1 Corinthians 12:5.

8. Colossians 3:23.

9. See Matthew 28:19 and Mark 16:15.

10. See 2 Timothy 1:5; 2:2.

11. Uncle Jimmy Graham was no relation to my family.

12. Pearl Buck, the 1938 winner of the Nobel Prize for literature, was an author who penned, among other books, *The Good Earth*, which won the Pulitzer Prize in 1931.

13. Ephesians 2:10.

14. See Zechariah 4:10.

15. See Acts 16:11–13.

16. I must confess that if I taught God's Word or preached the gospel for years on end and no one's life was ever changed, I would get on my face and ask God, *Why?* While the impact of ministry is His responsibility, I do expect some eternal fruit.

17. My paraphrase of Psalm 16:11.

EIGHT ∾ Stay Awake!

(pages 165–96)

1. Revelation 2:2–4.

2. 2 Timothy 1:6.

3. See Mark 1:35; 6:46, 47; Luke 3:21; 5:16; 6:12; 9:16, 18, 28; 11:1.

4. John Whittier, "Dear Lord and Father of Mankind," 1872.

5. This prayer-poem was written by Jill Briscoe for her session at the *Just Give Me Jesus* revivals. My thanks to her for granting me permission to reprint it here.

6. "Holy, Holy, Holy." Words by Reginald Heber, 1826. This classic hymn is based on Revelation 4:8–11.

7. See Isaiah 43:12.

8. See John 1:1–2, 14.

9. Isaiah 6:1–5.

10. See Psalm 66:18.

11. See 1 John 1:8, 10.

12. The word *confess* in 1 John 1:9 literally means to say the same thing about our sin that God says.

13. William Cowper, "There Is a Fountain Filled with Blood," 1771. The beautiful words to this hymn were inspired by Zechariah 13:1.

14. Horatio G. Spafford, "It Is Well with My Soul," 1873.

15. 1 John 1:9.

16. 1 John 1:7; Ephesians 1:7; Hebrews 10:4, 5, 10, 15, 17. I changed the pronouns to make them personal and put in my name.

17. Hebrews 10:19–22. I have slightly altered the wording to make it personal, and once again I've tucked my name into the text.

18. See John 6:44.

19. A great resource for prayer in this area is Patrick Johnstone, Robyn Johnstone, and Jason Mandryk, *Operation World,* 21st century ed. (Waynesboro, GA: Operation Mobilization, Paternoster Lifestyle, 2001).

20. John 3:16.

21. See 2 Corinthians 4:6.

22. See Matthew 24:14.

23. Matthew 11:28.

24. Isaiah 42:3.

25. Isaiah 61:1 – 3, which Jesus read in Luke 4:18 – 21.

26. Psalm 55:22.

27. Because ... if I never go through the fire of suffering, how will I ever know the full extent of God's glorious love and power when He shows up ... right in the midst of the flames?

28. I've changed the pronouns in the words of this hymn, "Dear Lord and Father of Mankind," by John G. Whittier, 1872.

29. According to *www. cyberhymnal.org,* the words to this beautiful hymn, "Be Still, My Soul," were written in 1752 by Katharina A. von Schlegel and translated from German to English in 1855 by Jane L. Borthwick.

30. See Revelation 21:4.

31. See Ephesians 1:17 – 19; 3:16 – 19; Colossians 1:9 – 12. Again, a few pronouns and other words have been adjusted to make the prayers of Paul more personal for you.

32. For specific ways to pray for me and for AnGeL Ministries, please go to our Website, www.AnneGrahamLotz. com, or sign up for our newsletter by writing to AnGeL Ministries, 5115 Holly Ridge Drive, Raleigh, NC 27612.

33. Acts 4:29.

34. See Matthew 6:13.

35. Daniel 9:17 – 19.

36. See 2 Timothy 3:5.

37. 2 Chronicles 7:14.

38. Isaiah 64:1.

39. I sincerely believe in teaching our children the Scriptures! But the way we do the instruction is critically important. So much is "caught" and not "taught." My mother quipped that you can't make your children like spinach, if every time they see you eating yours, you gag! In other words, we need to let our children "catch" us enjoying reading our Bibles and spending time on our knees in prayer if we expect them to do the same.

Epilogue

(pages 197 – 99)

1. Isaiah 57:15.

2. Hebrews 11:32 – 40.

3. See Ephesians 5:26 – 27.

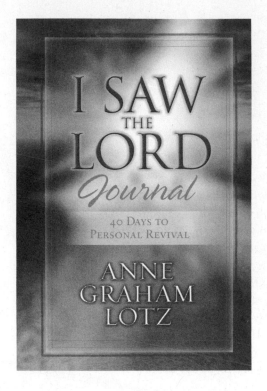

A companion prayer journal that provides
a framework for an ongoing prayer practice—
with prayer prompts, quotes, and Scriptures
—all carefully selected by Anne Graham Lotz
and tied to the theme of her book
I Saw the Lord.

ISBN 0-310-81154-6

Pick up a copy today at your favorite bookstore!

A Note to the Reader

After reading this book, if you need additional resources to help you maintain the fire of revival, please contact Anne Graham Lotz through one of the following means:

> AnGeL Ministries
> 5115 Hollyridge Drive
> Raleigh, NC 27612 – 3111
> 919 787-6606
> *www.AnneGrahamLotz.com.*
> Email inquiries: *info@angelministries.org*

We want to hear from you. Please send your comments about this book to us in care of zreview@zondervan.com. Thank you.

ZONDERVAN®

ZONDERVAN.com/
AUTHORTRACKER
follow your favorite authors